REVELATION

Other Volumes in the
SCRIPTURE FOR WORSHIP & EDUCATION
Series

Matthew

Mark

Luke

John

Acts of Apostles

*1 and 2 Corinthians
(forthcoming)*

Series edited by
Leonard Doohan

REVELATION

Proclaiming a Vision of Hope

Wilfrid J. Harrington, OP

Resource Publications, Inc.
San Jose, California

Editorial director: Kenneth Guentert
Managing editor: Elizabeth J. Asborno

Reprint Department
Resource Publications, Inc.
160 E. Virginia Street #290
San Jose, CA 95112-5876

Library of Congress Cataloging in Publication Data
Harrington, Wilfrid J.
   Revelation : proclaiming a vision of hope / Wilfrid J. Harrington.
       p.   cm. — (Scripture for worship & education series)
   Includes bibliographical references and indexes.
   ISBN 0-89390-307-8
   1. Bible. N.T. Revelation—Criticism, interpretation, etc.
I. Title. II. Series: Scripture for worship & education.
BS2825.2.H34 1994
228'.06—dc 20   94-35073

Printed in the United States of America

98 97 96 95 94 | 5 4 3 2 1

For
E. P. L.

’Ιδοὺ καινὰ ποιῶ πάντα

Revelation 21:5

Contents

Introduction

Bewilderment—that, in all likelihood, is the reaction of one who comes, for the first time, to the Book of Revelation. Those scrolls and plagues, those elders and living creatures, the dragon and the beasts—what can it be about? Is it any wonder that the book has become a happy-hunting ground for fundamentalists and for others who are mesmerized by prospect of the End? Is there any sense to be made of it? In truth, Revelation is a thoroughly Christian writing which, despite first impression, carries a message of startling hope.

One can, however, appreciate why it may disconcert. For, in the first place, it is not easy to classify Revelation. The work is certainly apocalyptic. Yet, its author is, professedly, a prophet; and he writes a letter. His text is open to more than one line of interpretation. Modern critical scholars agree on a proper approach to the work, insisting that it must be read in its own historical setting. Moreover, it is immediately evident that some appreciation of apocalyptic, some understanding of the literary genre apocalypse, is a prerequisite of any understanding of it. This will be the first concern of this book.

Revelation addresses a group of seven Christian communities in the late first-century CE (common era) Roman province of Asia (the western part of modern Turkey). The author, John, knows these churches thoroughly, and in his estimation, all is not well. He perceived a radical incompatibility between the Roman world of his day and the Gospel message. In his dualistic view, the perennial conflict between good and evil was being played out in terms of Rome and the Church. There were those Christians who did not share his assessment, those who sought accommodation. However, in his radical book, there was no place for compromise.

John had come to regard Rome as evil through and through. The Empire was instrument of the Dragon—Satan—implacable foe of the Lamb (Christ) and his followers. He was upset that some Christians did not see as clearly as he. He set out, then, to focus their attention on the true situation as he viewed it. He did so by demonizing Rome, by painting it in luridly negative colors. He sought to motivate his readers to reject Rome wholly. Their rejection will not be marked by violence; but it will be total. He had no illusion about the outcome. Rome will respond; there will be tribulation. John's was a minority position. First-century Christians, by and large, had learned to live with, and within, the Roman system. John stands as a challenge: a reminder, then and now, that the demands of Caesar may be in conflict with the claims of God.

Two figures dominate Revelation: the Almighty One on the heavenly throne, and the Lamb. The One on the throne displays his power in and through the Lamb who was slain. In his way, John makes the same point as Paul: "We proclaim Christ crucified... Christ the power of God and the wisdom of God" (1 Cor 1:23-24). So fully is the Lamb the manifestation and the very presence of God that, at the end of all, in the New

Jerusalem, in place of a temple is a single throne, "the throne of God and of the Lamb" (Rev 22:1).

In light of his challenge to his readers, with its call on their "patient endurance," a marked feature of John's work is encouragement and comfort. His encouragement is paradoxical. His model is the Lamb *who was slain*. The Lamb has pointed the way to victory: the Victim is the Victor. The Christian communities of John's concern are small groups, quite helpless before the might of Rome. There will be suffering and death. There will be victims. His encouragement is the assurance that those who are faithful unto death already rejoice, now and forever, with their Lord: "Blessed are the dead who die in the Lord henceforth" (14:13). Furthermore, threading through the book, one may discern the theme of universal salvation. Or, better expressed, that the *eschaton*, God's final word, is positive: salvation only. The message of Revelation is more than words of encouragement to those who suffer tribulation. It is promise of a wider hope.

Revelation is a letter that carries an explicit direction for its reading in liturgical assembly (1:3). It was designed to be *heard*. Somewhat as with radio-drama, the listener assimilates its words imaginatively. Spangled with heavenly liturgies, it sustains a liturgical dimension throughout. John's heavenly liturgies are, surely, echoes of community celebrations of his churches. Not surprisingly, there is echo of eucharistic celebration. All of this merits, and has received, special attention.

John wrote his letter to specific communities of his day and he addressed their situation—not ours. Still, he has a message for us. His radical stance challenges us to look more critically at the standards of our world. We must ask ourselves if we may not have, too readily, come to terms with the prevailing culture. He challenges our complacency. We do not need to be quite as uncompromising as John. But if we have the courage to look at our Christian situation through the prism of

3

the Gospel, we may observe more shadow than we are eager to acknowledge. Beyond the shadow shines steadfast hope. We may glimpse the New Jerusalem, the ultimate Rule of God—where God will be all in all. We may see the God of Justice—who wills the salvation of all. *Our* God is manifest in the Lamb. Our prayer is *Marana tha*—"Come, Lord Jesus!"

Chapter One

Introduction to the Book of Revelation

What Is Apocalypse?

Today we are not many years away from the year 2000. For some, the year 2000 is a magical date—irrespective of the fact that its computation is arbitrary. There is apocalyptic expectation. Biblical writings such as Ezekiel and especially Daniel and Revelation (Apocalypse) have long been a happy-hunting ground for fundamentalists. Approach of the magical year will fuel expectation of the End. We are surely going to be faced with many questions. One of these questions is: What is apocalypse?

The Meaning of Apocalypse

We have not only to define an already elusive word; we need to distinguish between "apocalypse," "apocalyptic eschatology" and "apocalypticism." A pedantic exercise, surely? Not so! We must know what we are talking about. And a lot of nonsense has been talked about apocalyptic—and not alone by fundamentalists.

Apocalypticism is not only a phenomenon of the past; it is a recurring religious phenomenon. It might well have more relevance in our day than perhaps we realize.

Let us come to grips with the terms. "Apocalypse" is a literary genre or form—the kind of literature in which apocalyptic views are expressed. "Apocalyptic eschatology" may best be understood in comparison with "prophetic eschatology." "Apocalypticism" is the world-view of an apocalyptic movement or group.

We turn first to prophetical eschatology. To put it very simply, the prophets of Israel, when they looked to the future, envisaged a future that would find form and shape in history. For instance, in the current of Davidic messianic expectation, it was thought that a glorious Davidic monarchy would eventually be established. Apocalyptists, for reasons which we shall see, had, largely, opted out of history. For them, there was no future in any human institution. The only hope was in a divine intervention which would radically challenge the status quo and, in fact, bring about a new situation involving the definitive vindication of the suffering elect. Apocalypticism is, in practice, a gospel of the marginalized. It proclaims: "God is on our side. Here we are—the minority, whether in relation to an alien power or in face of a power-group within our own society. 'We' have no clout. But right is on our side, and a God who looks not to might but to right has to be on our side." When one takes God seriously, it is a powerful argument. The question, of course, is whether one might make God to be whatever one wants God to be.

An apocalyptic group sets up its own symbolic universe; that is to say, it sets up a system of thought within which it can live its life. Usually, it does so in protest against the dominant society with which it is in conflict. The group has a painful experience of alienation, which may be due to a quarrel with the power group within its own society. Or, it may be a nation, or section of it, in protest against a system imposed by a foreign power. In either case there is the experience of powerlessness. Apocalyptists reject the dominant culture which they regard as irremediable. The current world is inherently, inescapably, evil. Hope lies in a divine intervention which will destroy the present evil age—and vindicate the alienated suffering ones. A favored manner of giving vent to the frustration and the hope was in writing; thus, we have the literary genre apocalypse.

Before offering a definition of apocalypse, it will help to see apocalyptic in relation to providence and eschatology. The word "providence" comes from the Latin *pro*, "before," and *videre*, "to see." Providence has to do with looking ahead, seeing what is before one. The providence of God means that God sees and directs the whole course of history. "Eschatology," from the Greek *eschaton*, "final," "the End," means that God is guiding history to a final goal. Apocalyptic affirms that God will bring about that final goal in the near future. His purpose has been secretly revealed (the Greek *apocalypsis* means "revelation") and will be made known. Disclosure of heavenly mysteries is an essential feature of apocalyptic.

The word "apocalypse" designates a type of Jewish literature which flourished about 200 BCE (before common era) to 100 CE. Apocalypse has been defined as:

> a genre of revelatory literature with a narrative framework in which revelation is mediated by an otherworldly being to a human recipient, disclosing a transcendent reality which is both temporal, insofar as it envisages eschatological salvation, and spatial insofar as it involves another, supernatural world (J. J. Collins, 4).

A brief analysis of the definition will clarify its content. The narrative framework of an apocalypse describes the manner of revelation. An apocalyptic seer claims to have been let into the secrets of the heavenly realm. He has access to heavenly secrets either by means of vision or audition (hearing the heavenly word) or through an otherworldly journey—in effect, a guided tour of heaven. A constant element is the presence of an *angelus interpres* ("interpreting angel") as interpreter or guide. This is to underline the fact that revelation alone is not enough; supernatural aid is required if one is to understand.

It is taken for granted that a supernatural world stands above our earthly world. That heavenly world is the "real" world. There is, indeed, a twofold dualism: vertical, the world above and our world, and horizontal, our age and the Age to come. In short, the presumption is of an otherworldly reality which dictates the fate of our world. There is a looking to life beyond death, a life very different from the life of our experience. In that future the apocalyptic group will be finally vindicated and come into their blessed home. There is always a definitive eschatological judgment: the final clash between Good and Evil, issuing in the total victory of God and the end of Evil.

Apocalyptic Writings

Apocalyptic developed in late Judaism. It will help to note that wider setting and indicate major Jewish apocalypses which have, directly or indirectly, influenced the author of Revelation.

The Book of Enoch (1 Enoch) is the oldest of three apocalyptic writings attributed to Enoch (Gen 5:18-24). It is a compilation of five "Books" or sections of unequal length and of differing dates—ranging from the third century BCE to before the end of the first century CE.

Chapters 1-36	The Book of the Watchers	3rd century BCE
Chapters 37-71	The Similitudes (Parables)	1st century CE
Chapters 72-82	The Astronomical Book	before 200 BCE
Chapters 83-90	The Book of Dreams	c. 165 BCE
Chapters 91-108	The Epistle of Enoch	200-175 BCE

In general, the work reflects the historical events preceding and following the Maccabean Revolt (167-164 BCE). It was to have a notable influence on early Christian tradition. For instance, the theme of fallen angels comes from the Book of the Watchers. The "Book" of the complex 1 Enoch offers something like a cross-section of the apocalyptic genre with its different literary forms. The tendency among scholars had been to view apocalypse only along the pattern of Revelation and Daniel 7-12. The truth is—as Enoch illustrates—that the apocalyptic message may be conveyed in various ways.

While Daniel 7-12 is unquestionably the first full-blown apocalypse in the Hebrew Bible (Daniel 1-6 being related stories), it is, most likely, not the oldest Jewish apocalypse. It would have been pre-dated by some of the Enochic material. Otherwise, Daniel 7-12 deserves to stand as the masterpiece of Jewish apocalyptic. It may even be dated with precision to 165 BCE—shortly before the death of Antiochus IV Epiphanes (the "villain" of Daniel). Daniel 7-12 consists of three visions (chapters 7, 8, 10-12) and a prophecy (chapter 9). Along the line, revelation is mediated by an angel. In each unit there is an historical pattern, an eschatological crisis, and the prospect of judgment and ultimate salvation.

In a series of visions, Daniel 7-12 traces the course of history, with stress on the ultimate, inevitable victory of the people of God. Daniel maintains that history is wholly under divine control. That is just the point. He tells the story of the past in such a way that the persecuted Jews may understand that their sufferings have a place in God's purpose. The book looks always to the final victory, to the time of the End, to the coming of the kingdom. It sees the messianic age about to dawn, beyond the time of tribulation. God's victory over the forces of evil is assured and those who serve him faithfully will have a glorious part in his triumph. Daniel, like apocalypse in general, presupposes the existence of a supernatural world above the visible one. The apocalyptic seer has an entree into the heavenly reality.

A common feature of apocalyptic also found in Daniel is determinism: there are two camps—the righteous and the wicked. And it is presupposed that there is little or no chance that the wicked will change allegiance. One must always keep in mind the cultural setting of apocalypticism. There is the powerless minority, effectively defranchised by the dominant group—who are not going to relinquish their powerbase. What can the oppressed do? The temptation to look toward a "soft" solution beyond death is rightly questioned in our day. The book of Daniel, however, does look only to a divine intervention. And it follows the road of determinism:

> Go your way, Daniel, for the words are to
> remain secret and sealed until the time of the
> end. Many shall be purified, cleansed, and
> refined, but the wicked shall continue to act
> wickedly. None of the wicked shall understand,
> but those who are wise shall understand
> (12:9-10).

This is an aspect of apocalypticism that needs to be faced and challenged. In Revelation John handles it by appeal to a prophetic insight.

The apocalypse 4 Ezra (2 Esdras) is a Jewish work written after the fall of Jerusalem (70 CE), about 90-120 CE. It is structured in seven scenes (dialogues and visions). We note points relevant to the study of Revelation. In the first vision (9:26-10:59), Ezra confronts a woman who grieves for the death of her only son. Abruptly, she turns into a city. An angel explains to Ezra that the woman was Zion and that God had shown him the glory of the future, restored Jerusalem (see Rev 21:9-14). The second vision (chapters 11-19) opens with the statement: "I saw an eagle coming up out of the sea; it had twelve feathered wings and three heads" (11:1). Here, the eagle is Rome; the heads are emperors. The eagle vision may be understood as a reinterpretation of the vision of the fourth beast of Daniel 7 (see Rev 13:17). The third vision (chapter 13) introduces "a figure like that of a man" (13:3) who "sent forth from his mouth as it were a stream of fire" (13:10). One is reminded of Revelation 19:15,21 ("the sword of his mouth"). The work known as 2 Baruch is closely related to 4 Ezra and is another response to Rome's conquest of Jerusalem. The problem faced is the prominence of evil in the world, especially in the shape of idolatry.

The genre of sibylline oracles had a long tradition—reaching back to the fifth century BCE—before it was adopted by Jews (and Christians). The *Sibylline Oracles* are extant in fourteen books (second century BCE to seventh century CE). They are not strictly apocalyptic, but they do have interest for a study of Revelation. Of special note is their use of the Nero legend. In the Roman world, there was widespread belief that Nero had not died (compare rumors of the survival of Hitler!) but had fled to the Parthians (the eastern threat to Rome) and would return, at the head of a Parthian army, to wreak vengeance on a Rome that had rejected him (*Nero redux*). Another, later, form of the legend had Nero return from the dead (*Nero redivivus*). John made use of the Nero legend (see Rev 13:3,12; 17:8-11).

These are but a few of the many apocalypses from before and about the time of Revelation. Because of unfamiliarity with the genre, apocalypse is, for us, strange, disturbing—when it is not wholly incomprehensible. We must realize that for John and his readers it would have been part of their culture. They would have understood its literary conventions and have heard its message. An apocalyptic writer is usually addressing what he perceives as a crisis situation. He is most anxious that his word be heard. He does not go out of his way to invent a bizarre form that would pass over the heads of his readers. Apocalypse was not at all as strange to those to whom it was first addressed as it has become for us.

The Book of Revelation

A Pastoral Letter to the Christians in Asia

Revelation is a letter (Revelation 1:4; 22:21) of a Christian prophet (1:3) addressed to a circle of Christian communities in towns of the Roman province of Asia (western Turkey). Apocalypse is crisis-literature. But, a small, vulnerable group can have a real experience of crisis in circumstances far from earth- shattering. By this time sharply distinct from the synagogue, these Christians could no longer shelter under the Jewish umbrella and avail of Roman tolerance of a *religio licita* (an officially approved religion—as Judaism was). The emperor-cult was an aggravating factor. Because they refused to pay token reverence to a deified emperor, they were classed (or might be classed) as disloyal citizens (or worse) and suffered, or might suffer, accordingly. Revelation is disturbing, but it carries its own Christian message. It is a reminder, radically expressed, that God will have the last word.

The author of Revelation obviously knows the Hebrew Bible thoroughly. He has, demonstrably, been heavily influenced by Daniel and Ezekiel. It can scarcely be doubted that he would have known some of the earlier or contemporary Jewish apocalyptic writings. While displaying a mastery of his bible, his use of scripture is free and creative. Not only does John never quote his Hebrew Bible sources, he frequently gives them a paradoxical twist. This creative literary freedom of John is a notable feature of his work. It is one reason why Revelation is such a fascinating text.

Four times (1:1,4,9; 22:8) the author of Revelation names himself: John. This is unusual. All other apocalypses we know of are pseudonymous—attributed to a personage of the past (such as Enoch or Ezra). While Christian tradition has, on the whole, identified him with John, son of Zebedee, the scholarly view, with good reason, does not concur. The best that can be said is that John is an otherwise unknown Christian prophet, most likely an itinerant prophet and, probably, a Palestinian by birth. The strongest external evidence for the date of Revelation is the testimony of Irenaeus: it was written in the reign of Domitian (81-96 CE). The clearest internal evidence is the use of the name "Babylon" for Rome. In Jewish literature this name is associated with Rome precisely as the second destroyer of Jerusalem (the first being the Babylonian king Nebuchadnezzar); its use indicates a date after 70 CE. We may, then, date Revelation approximately 90-95 CE.

It is well to keep in mind that Revelation was meant to be *heard*, to be listened to—"blessed are those who hear" (1:3). It has a dramatic dimension. One should note the oral flavor of it. Revelation is a pastoral letter to Christians in Asia, to be read aloud in the worship service of the communities (1:3). The churches of Asia were, in the main, Pauline churches. As a letter, influenced by the Pauline letter form, Revelation was written to specific Christians in a specific place, time and situation. It does not address us directly; we must first read and understand it in terms of its original readers. And if, so regarded, John has a message for our time, this is not to say that he makes predictions about our time.

It is not easy to classify Revelation. It is a mixed genre; it does not wholly conform to any known ancient literary convention. The work is certainly apocalyptic. Yet, its author is, professedly, a prophet, and he writes a letter. Revelation is, in short, a prophetic, apocalyptic letter addressed to specific Christian communities. The text is open to more than one line of interpretation. Modern critical scholars agree on the proper approach to the work. All insist that it must be read in its own historical setting. But they are not at one as to the nuances of its message.

A Community in Tribulation

While it was formerly claimed that the emperor Domitian was a prominent persecutor of Christians, there really is no evidence of widespread persecution in his time. Significantly, only one martyr is named in Revelation—Antipas (2:13). The book suggests, however, that John wrote in anticipation of universal persecution. Evidence firmly points to the fact that Christians, on the whole, lived peacefully in Asia. What does emerge, unmistakably, in Revelation is John's unequivocally negative attitude to the Roman Empire and to the Asian society that reflected the values of the Empire.

A pressing challenge to the faithful of Asia was the emperor-cult. The notion of the divinity of kings was an ancient and common one in the East; the practice was slower to find a foothold in Rome. Citizens of the eastern provinces were eager to raise temples to a divine Caesar. Refusal to accord the emperor divine honors could be considered an act of civil disloyalty or even treason. Christians in John's time and place might be subject to social and economic discrimination and harassment. This is not the same as all-out persecution.

John, a prophet, chose to write an apocalypse. It was a genre ideally suited to his purpose. It gave him full scope to paint the Empire in the most lurid colors. He could depict history as a stark struggle between the forces of Evil and the worshipers of God and of the Lamb. He could encourage his readers—encouragement is a constant feature of apocalypse. His encouragement was paradoxical. Victory was won on the cross. The enduring comfort is that the powerless victims will be, and will be seen to be, the ultimate victors. There is comfort rooted in realism. It is not John's last word. It is the *prophet* John (rather than the apocalyptist) who speaks the limitless graciousness of God.

Misinterpretation—A Problem for Contemporary Communities

Revelation is largely, if not exclusively, an apocalyptic work. From an early stage, it has been misunderstood; at least, there has been lack of appreciation of the literary form and imagery of apocalyptic. And there has been an unfortunate preoccupation with millennialism—an interpretation, often literal, of the thousand-year reign of Revelation 20:1-6. Down through the ages, the book has been subjected to varied and contradictory expositions.

One particular line of interpretation calls for some comment because of its prevalence. It might be termed the "futurist" interpretation. In this approach, Revelation is taken to be exclusively concerned with happenings at the close of the age. Even the seven churches of chapters 2-3 are not real churches of first-century

Asia but seven periods of Church history. The "dead" church of Laodicea becomes the apostate church of the interpreter's own time. The rest of the book looks to the end of the world and the events which will usher in the second coming of Christ. Since chapters 4-22 predict only those events that are to happen in the last years of world history, and since the interpreter stands at the threshold of the end, the whole book is meaningless not only for its first readers but for all subsequent generations up to the last.

Premillennial dispensationalism is a brand of fundamentalist eschatology which is notably prevalent in the United States. An indication of its popularity is the best-seller success of a book by Hal Lindsey: *The Late Great Planet Earth* (1970). This is, too, the position which underlies the preaching of the major contemporary TV evangelists. The term "dispensationalism" refers to the theory that God "dispenses" or administers the divine purpose throughout history in seven distinct and successive stages, called "dispensations." The seventh dispensation is that of the millennium (Rev 20:1-6). "Premillennial" distinguishes this view from other perceptions on the return of Christ at the close of history. Premillennialists believe that Christ will return *before* the millennium. After a brief reign of Antichrist, he will come, decisively to destroy the powers of evil in the great battle of Armageddon.

The concept of a millennium—perceived, literally, as a thousand-year reign with Christ on earth—and the final battle of Armageddon, show the influence of Revelation on the dispensationalist stance. History is rapidly moving to a showdown: the final, decisive battle of good and evil will be fought in the valley of Megiddo (Rev 16:16). A further refinement is the "rapture"; this time the single text of 1 Thessalonians 4:16-17 is pressed into service. Using vivid apocalyptic language, Paul had underlined the truth that all the faithful will live on with the Lord forever. He spoke of all being "caught up" ("rapt up") to meet the Lord at the parousia—hence the "rapture" of the dispensationalists. True believers will, at the end, be "raptured" from the earth and will thus escape the gruesome destruction of the rest of humankind.

Here we have not only gross misinterpretation of Revelation (and other biblical texts) but something unsavory and even dangerous. The idea of an elect minority being shunted to the safe regions of the upper air while a vengeful Lamb destroys the inhabitants of the earth is scarcely Christian. Politically, it could be maintained that world-wide nuclear war is really part of God's plan for his world. All of this is far removed from John's intent.

It is necessary to counter such serious misuse of a challenging biblical text. This book is a modest attempt to rescue Revelation by outlining its message and highlighting its contribution to Christian theology and practice.

An Outline of Revelation

The author of Revelation wrote idiosyncratic Greek. Some of his non-Greek idiom may be due to the fact that his native language was Semitic—most likely Aramaic (the language spoken by Jesus). But this cannot be the whole story; his peculiar grammar and syntax appear studied and not due to a poor grasp of Greek. It has been suggested that John wrote as he did in conscious protest against Hellenistic culture. The distinctive style pervades the book—a factor in the cumulative argument that speaks for a unified, structured work. This is not to say that it is easy to discern the precise structure intended by John. There are unmistakable features, notably, reference to three scrolls (1:11; 5:1; 10:1); and four septets: messages (chapters 2-3), seals (6:1-8:1), trumpets (8:2-11:9) and bowls (chapters 15-16). There have been many attempts to trace an elaborate sequence throughout. While the book is surely not shapeless, it seems that little is to be gained by imposing a logical plan on a work of such imaginative power and such deep religious feeling. It is more helpful to propose an outline of the book, one which may suggest a line of interpretation.

Overture (Chapter 1)

The prologue (1:1-3) introduces Revelation as a letter from the prophet John to be publicly read at community worship—a letter addressed to seven churches in the Roman province of Asia (1:4-8). A blessing of grace and peace issues from God—a God especially active and present in Jesus Christ. His titles, "the faithful witness, the firstborn of the dead, and ruler of the kings of earth" (1:5), speak to the situation of John's readers: fidelity unto death, victor over death, God's answer to Caesar's arrogance. He is example and source of hope for Christians about to face the great persecution. Jesus' help is not only for the future; it is, more intimately, in the past and in the present. We were sinners; he liberated us from the evil actions and deeds of our past—by dying on our behalf. He has raised us to royalty: a royal house of priests, inheriting the privilege of the chosen people.

In a striking vision (1:9-20) John received his prophetic commission. He is commanded to write what is to be revealed to him and send the message to seven churches of Asia. On the island of Patmos, on the Lord's day, he had a vision of "one in human form": the glorified Christ who walked among the seven lamps (the churches) and held in his right hand (in his power) seven stars, the heavenly counterparts of the churches. He is no absentee landlord. This inaugural vision effectively brings out the oracular character of the first part of Revelation (chapters 1-3) for it is closely parallel to the inaugural visions of the Hebrew Bible prophets (see Isa 6). But where the latter proceeded to speak in the name of Yahweh, John will make known the "revelation of Jesus Christ."

Prophetic Messages (Chapters 2-3)

In the messages, each of seven churches hears a verdict based on precise knowledge of its situation, both external (there are topical references) and spiritual. The churches receive praise or blame (or both), usually with some qualifications. Ephesus (2:1-7) receives both censure and commendation. The praiseworthy works are its "toil" in resisting and overcoming false teachers and its "patient endurance," for the sake of Christ, in the labors and trials of the effort. Though the Ephesian Christians had maintained orthodoxy, their love had waned. It may be that their zeal for truth pushed them too far and proved the cause of their failure to love. The tribulation and poverty of faithful Smyrna (1:8-11) are noted as well as that church's special problem of Jewish hostility. Christians had claimed to be the true Israel, a claim not welcome to ethnic Jews!

The church of Pergamum (1:12-17) holds out bravely in a center of emperor-worship; but the Nicolaitans (Christians who disagreed with his view), John's bugbear, have made inroads. The church of Pergamum was under pressure of more than one kind. Devotees of emperor-worship looked askance at these "disloyal" and subversive people. One of them, Antipas, had paid the ultimate price. To John's eyes more serious was betrayal within—in his view any compromise with the prevailing culture was betrayal. The community of Thyatira (1:18-29), otherwise exemplary, tolerates a Christian teacher who proposed adaptation to the prevailing ethos, a proposal anathema to the prophet. This is "Nicolaitanism." At stake was the question of assimilation: To what extent might Christians conform to the prevailing culture for the sake of economic survival or social acceptance? For John the only answer was: Not at all!

The church of Sardis (3:1-6) is in poor shape; it lacks backbone. The Christians of Sardis are either spiritually dead or in spiritual torpor. Life is not quite extinct; but these Christians must come fully awake and carefully tend the spark of life that does remain, lest it should really be extinguished. The lamentable state of the church is displayed in its half-hearted living of the Christian life. Philadelphia (3:7-13), a poor, humanly powerless community, merits unstinted praise. As at Smyrna, a particular problem of Christians at Philadelphia was Jewish hostility. In contrast to Smyrna, there is promise of the conversion of the Jewish opposition in Philadelphia. Here only, in relation to this little but faithful church, we find explicit mention of the love of Christ: "I have loved you" (3:9).

The opulent church in the prosperous town of Laodicea (3:14-22) fares badly; about this community alone the heavenly scrutineer has nothing good to say. These Christians are lukewarm, neither hot nor cold. They must not only repent but "be zealous" (3:19), shake themselves out of their lethargy. At the end the Lover turns (v 20) from the church to the individual Christian and seeks an entry into the human heart. The true disciple will hear the voice of his or her friend. There is a eucharistic flavor to the promise of a meal shared by Christ and the Christian (v 20).

The messages to the churches should be kept in mind throughout the visions that follow. The communities to and for whom John writes are communities of real men and women, of people who are coping, not always effectively, with difficult and painful situations. Though John might seem to live in a fantasy world, his concern is focused on these troubled churches. His purpose is firmly pastoral.

The Scroll Vision (Chapters 4-5)

The opening vision of the throne of God (chapter 4) is manifestly inspired by several prophetic texts, notably the inaugural vision of Ezekiel (Ezek 1-3). John has been rapt to heaven and, for the rest of the book, he will be predominantly concerned with heavenly visions and auditions. The first object that catches John's eye is a throne, symbol of divine sovereignty. Before the throne the "twenty-four elders" are heavenly counterparts of the earthly people of God; the "four living creatures" represent all aspects of created life. In a great liturgy the whole of creation sings praise of the Creator (Rev 4:8-10).

In chapter 5 the "One seated on the throne"—designation of God throughout—handed over to the Lamb the sealed scroll which he held in his right hand: a transfer of power. It is a *sealed* scroll. The breaking of the seals is a special, indeed an exclusive, task which the Lamb alone can perform. "I wept bitterly" (5:4): John weeps because there is no human agent to set God's purpose for humankind in train; he had understood that God will not dispense with an agent, such is his respect for humankind. One of the elders comforts John by assuring him that all is well. "Then one of the elders said to me...the Lion of the tribe of Judah...has conquered....I saw a Lamb standing, as though it had been slain" (5:5-6). In his vision John looked for the emergence of a Lion—and saw a slaughtered Lamb! What he learned, and what he tells his readers, is that the Lion *is* the Lamb; the ultimate power of God ("lion") is manifest on the cross ("lamb"). This is why "Lamb" is John's definitive name for Christ. The heavenly hymns in praise of the Lamb (5:9-13) serve to interpret the vision.

The Seven Seals (6:1-8:5)

The breaking of the scroll-seals by the Lamb un-leashed a series of plagues which follows the pattern of events in the Synoptic apocalypse (Mt 24; Mk 13; Lk 21): war, strife among nations, famine, pestilence, persecution, cosmic phenomena. The first four seals (6:1-8) are the celebrated "four horsemen of the Apoca-lypse"—war and its attendant evils. The fifth seal (6:9-11) introduces martyrs resting underneath the heav-enly altar—they are sacrificial victims. God will vindicate them by demonstrating, clearly, unmistak-ably, that evil has not won. It will become evident to all that these helpless victims are the true, the only vic-tors. At the breaking of the sixth seal appear the traditional cosmic signs that presage the End (6:12-17). Before the breaking of the last seal the servants of God were sealed with the seal of the living God (7:1-8), sealed for protection *through* the great tribulation—144,000, the Israel of God. In 7:9-17 they, beyond the tribulation, celebrate victory in a heavenly feast of Tabernacles. The vision is proleptic—it anticipates the triumph of the faithful ones. The seventh seal (8:1-5) marks an end which is also a beginning: it heralds a fresh series of plagues (8:6-11:19). While Revelation never directly refers to the liturgy of the earthly Church, Christians would surely recognize their prayers in the incense rising before the heavenly throne (8:4).

The Seven Trumpets (8:6-11:9)

The trumpets—modeled on the plagues of Egypt—are presented in much the same manner as the Seals: the first four are described in a few verses (8:6-13); the others unfold at greater length, interspersed with other visions. The plagues, triggered by the trumpet blasts, strike *one third* of earth and heaven—contrast the "fourth of the earth" of the Seals. It is Act 2 of the drama: Act 1 repeated with more dramatic intensity. In his series of plagues John is not indulging in tiresome repetition; he is building up to a dramatic climax. He is leading to *the* ultimate battle, the decisive conflict between Good and Evil. The triple woe (8:13) has reference to the three remaining trumpet-blasts or, more precisely, to the visitations called forth by them.

The fifth trumpet (or first woe) depicts a plague of demonic locusts (9:1-12)—an Egyptian-style plague of locusts already greatly embellished by Joel (see Ex 10:12-18; Joel 1:6-7; 2:1-11). The locusts symbolize the oppressive burden of evil that weighs on our world. The sixth plague (second woe) shows vast demonic forces from beyond the Euphrates, bent on the destruction of Rome (9:13-21). The motivation of the plagues is not vindictiveness; they are a summons to *metanoia*. But, as with Pharaoh, this purpose was not achieved: humankind did not repent.

Chapter 10 opens with a vision of a mighty angel holding a little scroll open in his hand: a fresh prophetical commission. It is an "open scroll"—the time of waiting is over. The angel's words in 10:8-10 are inspired by Ezekiel 3:1-3, a prophetic investiture; the eating of the scroll symbolizes the prophet's digesting of the message which he has to transmit. Before morning there is the pre-dawn darkness of the final tribulation (chapter 11). Pagans will tread down the holy city for 1,260 days (a variant of the three-and-a-half years of Daniel: a limited period of tribulation before final vindication) but the temple and those worshiping in it will be spared (11:1-2). The Church as such will stand; Christians must suffer the ordeal. Throughout the time of tribulation the two witnesses (11:3-14), representing the Church in its function of witness-bearing, will exercise their prophetic ministry. Slain by the power of evil, they will be vindicated by God and restored to life. They mirror the destiny of the Lamb.

The seventh trumpet, which follows without delay the announcement of the third woe (v 14), may perhaps be that third woe (11:15-19). It is a prophetic judgment scene. The time has come for judging, for rewarding, and for destroying. Again in anticipatory vision the holy of holies of the heavenly temple is thrown open and the ark of the covenant is visible to all (11:19). The fulfillment will be in the New Jerusalem when God will dwell with humankind (21:3).

The Woman and the Dragon (Chapter 12)

Chapters 12 and 13 offer a behind-the-scenes view of the power of evil at work in the present; chapter 14 offers an anticipated view of the victory of God in salvation and judgment. Chapter 12 combines a narrative describing an encounter between a pregnant woman and a dragon (vv 1-6,13-17) with a narrative depicting a heavenly battle (vv 7-9). This sandwich-technique, reminiscent of Mark, indicates that the narratives must be understood in conjunction. The woman symbolizes the people of God bringing forth the Messiah; the dragon is the "ancient serpent" of Genesis 3. By the "birth" of the Messiah (12:5) John does not mean the nativity but the cross—the enthronement of Jesus. The woman's child was snatched from the destructive intent of the dragon to the throne of God: precisely by dying, Jesus defeated the dragon and was exalted to God's right hand. The expulsion of Satan from heaven is the result of the victory of Christ on earth; this is clearly brought out in the heavenly chorus of 12:10-11. Though defeated in heaven, evil still finds scope on earth. While the Church, as such, is under God's special care (12:6,14), the faithful are vulnerable (12:17). This story, it should be said, is not concerned with the origin of "Satan" and has nothing to do with a mythological fall of angels.

The Two Beasts (Chapter 13)

The two beasts of chapter 13, instruments of the dragon, are, respectively, Rome and the propagators of the imperial cult. John's first beast (13:1-10), emerging from the sea, is a composite of the four beasts of Daniel 7:2-8—it is the epitome of evil. To this beast (Rome) the dragon (Satan) gave his power and authority. The beast is a parody of the Lamb; the healing of its mortal wound is reference to the Nero legend. It is not only enemy of God; it is enemy of humankind.

The second beast (13:11-17), later called the "false prophet," who induces all the "inhabitants of the earth" to worship the first beast, is the imperial religion in the service of Rome. For John the second beast represented false religion, specifically the emperor-cult. Historically, even religion that is "authentic" has too often worn aspects of the beast.

Salvation and Judgment (Chapter 14)

In deliberate and striking antithesis to the beast and its followers stand the Lamb and his followers (14:1-5). The characterization of the Lamb's companions as "they who have not defiled themselves with women" rings offensively. It is likely that the designation "virgins" should be understood in a metaphorical sense; in the prophets, idolatry was described as adultery or fornication. The 144,000 are contrasted with the followers of the beast because they have refused to worship the beast and have remained faithful to the Lamb. In not giving themselves to the cult of the beast they have kept their virginity.

Satan, the beasts and their followers ("the inhabitants of the earth"), the woman and her children, the Lamb and his companions—the dramatis personae of the eschatological struggle—have been introduced. Next comes the proclamation of the hour of judgment

(14:6-13) which is, paradoxically, proclamation, too, to the whole earth, of an "eternal gospel" (14:6), which can only mean *the* gospel. All humankind is urged to "fear God and give him glory" (14:7)—a call to repentance, to *metanoia*. In 14:9-12 there is threat of judgment; in contrast a heavenly voice assures the faithful ones that they are about to enter into rest (v 13).

The picture of harvest and vintage (14:14-20) is based on Joel 3:12-13—the extermination of the pagan nations. Undoubtedly, for Joel, harvest and vintage are parallel images of judgment. John, in his customary manner, has reacted freely to his source and has developed differently (harvest = salvation, vintage = judgment) each part of the Joel couplet. The one "like a son of man" (14:14) is Christ come to gather his elect. The angel of verse 18 is angel of judgment. The passage Isaiah 63:1-6 suggests the great wine-press of the wrath of God. It does not follow that John (14:19-20) employs the imagery in its original sense. He understands the "wrath" of God as God's radical incompatibility with evil.

The Last Plagues (Chapters 15-16)

The seven plagues *which are the last* (15:1) are announced in chapter 15; the following chapter shows their execution. Modeled, like the trumpets, on the plagues of Egypt, the bowls follow the pattern of a rapid unfolding of the first four (16:1-9). This time, however, chastisement is universal and definitive: all followers of the beast are stricken. In the heavenly scene of 15:1-4 the victors chant their victory song. Though termed "song of Moses," their song, unlike the song of Exodus (Ex 15:1-18), is not one of triumph over enemies: it is solely praise of God. John sees, coming from the heavenly sanctuary, seven angels carrying the bowls of God's wrath. He surely invites us to view the plagues about to be unleashed (15:5-8) against the background of a God who thinks only of salvation (15:3-4).

The first five plagues follow in quick succession (16:2-9). While not even those final plagues deny an opportunity to repent, the worshipers of the beast are obdurate. In 16:12-16 (sixth bowl) the followers of the beast are gathered at Armageddon, symbol of disaster and figure of the eschatological battle (see 19:17-21). The final plague, the seventh (16:17-21), is of cosmic range; so the seventh angel poured his bowl "into the air" (16:17). The seven plagues of the bowls are "the last." As the plagues of Egypt were meant to bring Pharaoh to relent, to "let my people go," these plagues of bowls are a final effort to bring people to repent. In chapter 16 the focus narrows from the cosmos to the representative of the world's rebellion against the Creator—Rome—leading to the climactic chapters 17-19.

The Harlot and the Beast (Chapter 17)

Although the fall of Rome is proclaimed in 14:8 and is briefly described in 16:19, the end of that city, the great persecuting power, cannot be treated so casually. The whole of chapter 17 is given over to a description of Babylon—the goddess Rome—seated on the satanic beast; the fall of Rome is solemnly acclaimed in 18:1-8. The plagues of bowls were the last; what follows on them fills out the details of these plagues. An *angelus interpres* lists the significant details of the vision: the woman, the beast, his seven heads and his ten horns. In his explanation he takes the beast first (17:8-17) and briefly mentions the harlot last of all (v 18). John again bends the Nero legend to his purpose. The beast is said to have died of its wound ("is not") and gone to the abyss, and it has returned but only to go to final doom (17:7-11; see 19:20). The eighth emperor, "one of the seven"—another Nero—is the last sinister embodiment of evil. The ten kings, with the beast, turn on Rome

(17:16-17) and make war on the Lamb—to their own destruction (17:14; see 19:11-21).

The End of Babylon (18:1-19:10)

The fall of Babylon is solemnly proclaimed in 18:1-8. John lingers over the fate of Rome. He had devoted chapter 17 to a description of "Babylon," ending with assurance of its destruction. Now he develops that oracle of doom against the "great city." The reason for Babylon's punishment is, in the first place, her idolatry. But there is also the luxury of the city. The Christians of Asia are bidden "come out" of Rome by resisting the culture and values of the Empire. The fall of Rome finds dramatic expression in the three dirges chanted over her conflagration—self-interested laments of kings, merchants, and sea-farers who had battened on the extravagant wealth of Rome.

Verse 20, which anticipates the canticle of 19:1-8, introduces the symbolic judgment (v 21) and the heavenly lament (vv 22-24). Now, "saints and apostles and prophets," who have come triumphantly through the great tribulation engineered by Satan, join in the heavenly rejoicing. Their suffering has made the heavenly victory an earthly reality. The solemn repetition of the phrase "will be...no more" (18:22-23) gives an air of pathetic finality to the fate of Rome.

A heavenly liturgy (19:1-10) celebrates the vindication of God's people. A voice from the throne (19:5) summons all servants of God to praise the Lord: the vast throng of victors takes up the hymn. The victors are invited guests at the marriage feast of the Lamb (19:7-9). John, overwhelmed by a vision which bore the seal of divine authority, spontaneously fell at the feet of the angel. This angel firmly declares himself a fellow-servant: angels do not outrank Christians. The passage seems to be a warning against angel worship (19:10; see 22:8-9).

The End of Evil (19:11-20:15)

The passage 19:11-21 deals with the victory of Christ
and his followers over the beast, the false prophet, and
the kings of the earth. Victory is achieved by a majestic
Rider, wearing a cloak "dipped in blood" whose public
name is "Word of God" (19:13). The Victor is red with
his own blood rather than with that of his enemies: it
is victory of the slain Lamb. Victory is complete: the two
beasts are cast into the "lake of fire"—symbol of final
destruction—and their followers are slain.

In 20:1-10 we have two events juxtaposed: on the
one hand is the overthrow of Satan, in two phases; on
the other there is a reign of a thousand years. While
Christ and his faithful reign, Satan will be powerless
in their regard. The binding of Satan coincides with his
downfall described in the parallel passage 12:7-12. He
has no power over those who have "conquered him by
the blood of the Lamb" (12:11). The picture of the
millennium is only one of John's ways of thinking about
the End. It is wrong-headed to see it out of focus.

Inspired by Ezekiel (chapter 39), John (20:7-10)
presents a picture of the final struggle of evil: Gog and
Magog are larger-than-life antagonists of God. In order
to participate in this mythical scene the devil "must"
be released to engage in his characteristic activity of
"deceiving the nations." Then, defeated, Satan joins the
two (symbolic) beasts in the lake of fire. The conquest
of all powers hostile to God is followed by the general
resurrection of the dead and the last judgment (20:11-
15). In the judgment scene John contrasts "books" and
the "book of life" (20:12). People are judged by what
they had done; yet, what is ultimately decisive is
whether one's name is inscribed in the book of life.
John sought to present, on the one hand, the frightful
human responsibility of the decision to reject one's
Creator and live in servitude to false gods, and, on the
other hand, to portray the final victorious mercy of a

gracious God. With the total disappearance of evil, the present world order has come to an end.

The New Jerusalem (21:1-22:5)

The former creation has passed away and all evil has been destroyed; now is the final phase of God's plan. The book closes with a magnificent vision of the New Jerusalem, the heavenly city. One of the seven angels of the bowls had shown John the great harlot (17:1); one of the seven now steps forward to show him the bride (21:9). The bride image, however, is not developed but leads to that of the holy city (21:9-27). The twelve gates of the city are inscribed with the names of the twelve tribes of Israel; its twelve foundation-stones bear the names of the twelve apostles of the Lamb (21:12,14). John maintains the continuity of Israel and the Christian Church. In verses 24-26 it is declared that the gates remain always open, inviting the entry of the nations; all traffic is *into* the city (vv 24,26,27).

We might expect the glowing description of the city to be followed by a particularly striking description of its temple (the temple was the glory of the earthly Jerusalem). Instead, a brilliant touch, we learn that there is no temple, nor any need of one: God himself dwells there with the Lamb. Now indeed, "God's dwelling is with humankind" (21:3) and the glory of his presence pervades the whole city (vv 11,18), making the New Jerusalem, City of God, one vast Temple. Consistently, the waters which in Ezekiel 47 (the model text) flow from the temple, here flow from "the throne of God and of the Lamb" (22:1). It is the river of the first paradise, and the tree of life is found again (see Gen 2:9-10). There, the elect will look upon the face of God and of the Lamb and will reign for ever and ever.

An epilogue (22:6-20) gives the closing words of the angel, the seer, and the Lord. John ends his work with the prayer of the early Christians: *Marana tha* ("Our Lord, Come!") and with a parting blessing on *all* (22:21).

For Personal and Group Reflection

1. John had come to regard the empire as evil through and through. How do you regard the relationship between religion and the state?

2. Revelation is a call to encouragement, comfort, and patient endurance in face of the oppression against religion. In what ways do you experience oppression in the practice of religion? How can the group or parish community encourage and comfort each other in faithfulness?

3. John challenges the complacency of the so-called devout, calling them to examine more critically the standards of the prevailing culture. What aspects of our everyday lives need to be reexamined? Where can we adapt the faith? Where should we be uncompromising?

4. Revelation is a happy-hunting ground for fundamentalists. Are there any fundamentalist features of your faith—biblical, doctrinal, spiritual, papalist?

5. Apocalyptists find no hope in any human institution. What is your approach to human institutions? Do they give you any reason for hope?

6. Do you think apocalyptists are escapists? Why or why not?

7. A common feature of apocalyptic thought is the division of people into two camps, the righteous and the wicked. Where do you find signs of this today? Who do you think would be examples of self-styled "apocalyptic seers" in recent years?

8. Revelation is "crisis literature," written in anticipation of universal persecution. Do you think Christianity faces persecution today? Where? From outside the churches or from within?

9. Give some present-day examples of the misuse and misinterpretation of Revelation.

10. What are your personal and group expectations as you begin the reading of the Book of Revelation?

Chapter Two

John's Purpose

J ohn was a Jewish Christian, quite likely a
Palestinian Jew by birth. Like Paul before him
he had found in Jesus Christ his way to God.
He had seen in Jesus the very image of his God. Paul
had founded Christian communities in the Roman
province of Asia. Now these and later communities are
the concern of John. Even in one province of the Roman
Empire they were a small minority and, politically,
quite helpless. The tide of the Roman world flowed
steadily against them. That was bad enough. He was
more concerned that there were some among them who
felt that they might swim with the tide. This explains,
in part, the vehemence of his imagery and language.

John saw, with prophetic conviction, that something
was rotten at the heart of Rome. His preoccupation with
Rome is understandable: the Roman Empire was the
world of his day. For that matter, the Empire was the
world of all Christian Scripture writers. As far as they
were concerned, nothing existed beyond the Empire.
John's vision is firmly dualistic: there is God, and there
is Evil. In his eyes, Rome was wholly evil. Not all
Christians saw it so. We have the evidence of the
pastoral letters (1 and 2 Timothy; Titus).

Christianity and Rome

Other Christian Scripture Writers' Views of Rome

Evaluation of Pastorals (1 and 2 Timothy; Titus) must take into account the change in the way the Church understood itself. The Church must make adjustments for a prolonged stay in the world. The author (though attributed to Paul, these letters were written much later than the time of Paul) seeks to build, on Christian principles, a life in this world; he wishes to be part of the world. Thus, for him, the peace of a serene life is the goal of the Christian. "I urge that supplications, prayers, intercessions, and thanksgivings be made for everyone, for kings and all who are in high positions, so that we may lead a quiet and peaceable life in all godliness and dignity" (1 Tim 2:1-2). Prayer for the Roman authority was a synagogue practice. Paul also testifies to loyalty to the state and its officials (Rom 13:1-7). These Pastoral Christians had come to terms with the world in which they lived. They were to be model citizens of that world. Theirs is an eminently sensible Church, concentrating on structure, orthodoxy and respectability. It is the sort of Church with which we are familiar because, historically, the Christian Church has followed the pastoral model.

The author of Pastorals asked that Christians should be good citizens. "Good citizen" may be an ambiguous label. Much depends on why the label is affixed. It can imply passive acceptance of institutions that are, in fact, sinful. There is no doubt that from the standpoint of institution, passive citizens are very "good citizens" indeed. John's assessment was categorically clear and wholly contrary to the Pastoral view. This is not to say that John actually knew any such Christians. But he surely was aware that other Christians did not see the situation in the same way as he. Something had to be done. He decided to write. Given the prevailing culture and the urgency of the situation as he perceived it, he wrote an apocalypse.

John's View of Rome

John's is a minority position. First-century Christians had, by and large, learned to live with and within the Roman system. John stands as a challenge—a reminder, then and now, that the demands of Caesar may be in conflict with the claims of God. John perceives a radical incompatibility between the Roman world and the Gospel message. In his dualistic view, the perennial conflict between good and evil is being played out in terms of Rome and Church. Christians may not, in any measure, be followers of the beast. He proposes his view with prophetic singlemindedness and apocalyptic exuberance. Yet, in doing so, he seems to be motivated by a singularly un-Christian vindictiveness—the awesome plagues and the ultimate merciless extermination of "the inhabitants of the earth." We will, later, come to a re-estimation of this factor.

The communities of John's concern are not victims of relentless persecution. He, rather, prepares his readers for the reaction that must inevitably follow his proposed defiance of Rome. Revelation continues to offer encouragement to all who find themselves in conflict with an ethos that is inimical to the standard of the gospel.

Rome Demonized

As a prophet, John could not settle for half measures. He viewed all authority based on power as demonic. The civil authority of his day, the Roman imperium, was, without doubt, based on power. And the authority was bolstered by a sycophantic religious system. The whole setup, in his eyes, was demonic. Surely history has substantiated that John's assessment of power structures is not too wide of the mark. He wrote to and for Christian communities. He clearly perceived the threat to Christians that is constituted by a worldly authority pattern.

John faced an uphill battle. Some—likely many— even in the Asian communities of his concern, had come to terms with the Roman world. He had, then, a two-fold reason for his assault on Rome. In the first place, there was his own conviction that imperial Rome was an instrument of Satan. Secondly, he had to persuade his fellow-Christians to think again about their willingness to work within the contemporary social system. He felt that he had, even, to turn them from their admiration of features of that world. On both scores his depiction of Rome was negative in the extreme. He could not find a good word to say in favor of the Empire.

Besides, he was convinced that Rome carried, within itself, the seed of its own destruction. Despite its appearance of invincibility, the Empire was fatally brittle. Furthermore, because he shared the widespread early Christian expectation of an imminent End, he believed that the fall of the Empire would be soon. It would surely be utterly foolish for any Christian to place trust in a regime that was sick unto death.

There was even more to it. The fall of Rome would be presage of the End. A Christian concern should be to hasten the dissolution of the evil empire. This did not, by any means, call for violent action. Rejection should be total; resistance must be passive. The reason is that, paradoxically, victory is won through defeat! The Victim is the Victor. Even passive resistance, however, will inevitably incite the reaction of Rome; a power-based authority can brook no dissension. John urged his Christians to resistance. He expected to be heeded and so could warn insistently and repeatedly of tribulation. As disciples of the slain Lamb, Christians cannot expect to be greater than the Master.

The apocalyptic genre suited John's purpose admirably. It gave him all the scope he wished to paint the Empire in the most lurid colors. He could depict a dramatic struggle between the forces of Evil and the worshipers of God and the Lamb. Encouragement is a constant feature of apocalyptic; he would encourage his readers. Because victory was won on the cross his encouragement was paradoxical. Faithful Christians will surely shed their blood. His encouragement lay not in conjuring up false hope of miraculous intervention but by reinterpreting the suffering of Christians. It was not to be doubted that the beast could, and would, strike mercilessly, savagely. The enduring comfort is that the helpless victims will be, and will be seen to be, the ultimate victors. There is comfort rooted in realism.

The apocalyptic denouement is not John's last word. The kings of the earth and the inhabitants of the earth slain in the great battle (19:19-21) will march confidently through the welcoming gates of the New Jerusalem! (21:24-26) This paradox calls for special attention.

John's Vision of Universal Salvation

If John were only an apocalyptist, he might have settled for the conventional scenario. In that case, the faithful followers of the Lamb, and they alone, would have a place in the New Jerusalem. He knows his God better than that. Throughout he is careful to distinguish between the "destroyers of the earth" and the "inhabitants of the earth." The former, the dragon and the two beasts, are symbols of pervasive evil. The others are deluded humans, swayed by evil. The plagues are not only an expression of God's incompatibility with sin and evil, they are aimed at the repentance of the victims of evil. John's Christian faith in the mercy and saving power of God inspired him to sustain a chain of startling "inconsistencies." He never forgot that his foolish God will have the last word.

Some have found in Revelation a doctrine of universal salvation. At first blush, suggestion of such a presence must seem absurd; Revelation displays such a spirit of vindictiveness and revels so in the destruction of earth and its inhabitants that it can scarcely be taken for a Christian book. Closer study, based on an understanding of the genre and of the purpose of the writing as well as of the strong prophetic element, does lead one to a different assessment.

Universal Salvation

If salvation means fellowship with God and blessedness of eternal life with him, universal salvation means that all human beings will finally be redeemed by God's gracious love—a love displayed ultimately in Jesus Christ. On the other hand, a limited salvation view assumes that only those who, in this life, acknowledge the true God—and, in the Christian Scripture setting, confess Christ as Lord—will finally be saved. Both views—limited salvation and universal salvation—are found prominently presented in both Hebrew Scripture and Christian Scripture. A stream of texts maintains that ultimate salvation is limited (e.g., Isa 26:20-21; 66:15-16; Mt 25:31-46; Jn 3:36). Another stream suggests or affirms universal salvation (e.g., Isa 66:18-23; Jn 3:17; Rom 11:32-36; 1 Tim 2:3-4). In some cases— and this is significant for an assessment of Revelation—both views are juxtaposed. For example, Isaiah says,

> For the LORD will come in fire...
> to pay back his anger in fury....
> For by fire will the LORD execute judgment,
>   and by his sword, on all flesh;

> and those slain by the LORD shall be many
> (Isa 66:15-16).

Immediately afterward, 66:18-23, we read:

> I am coming to gather all nations and tongues;
> and they shall come and shall see my glory, and
> I will set a sign among them. From them I will
> send survivors to the nations...to the coastlands
> far away that have not heard of my fame or seen
> my glory; and they shall declare my glory among
> the nations.

Or again, John 3:36: "Whoever believes in the Son has eternal life; whoever disobeys the Son will not see life, but must endure God's wrath." This stands in sharp contrast to the statement a few verses earlier (3:17): "Indeed, God did not send the Son into the world to condemn the world, but in order that the world might be saved through him."

Arguably, the weightiest text of all in favor of universal salvation is found in Paul. One may well find that Romans 9-11 is not the easiest section of Paul's writings. But one cannot fail to be stirred by the passion behind these pages. Paul simply will *not* accept that God has rejected his people (Rom 11:1). His argument throughout is tortuous, because the problem he addresses is so puzzling: How could God's people have failed to recognize God's last Messenger? He wrestles, despairingly, with a humanly incomprehensible situation, but he never loosens his grip on his conviction that "the gifts and the calling of God are irrevocable" (11:29). At the end, he commits the whole matter to God and declares, in words that have little to do with the forced logic of his argument up to now: "and so all Israel will be saved" (11:26)—a remarkable statement. Then Paul takes a truly giant step: "For God has imprisoned all in disobedience so that he may be merciful to all" (11:32). His declaration has to be seen

39

in contrast to the unrelieved picture he had painted in chapters 1-3—all humankind stands under sin, cut off from God. But, then, that backdrop was designed to highlight the incredible graciousness of God.

Turning to Revelation, we find here, as elsewhere, texts which imply or assert limited salvation (e.g., 14:9-10; 20:11-15) and texts which imply or assert universal salvation (e.g., 1:7; 5:13; 14:6-7; 21:24-27). While this juxtaposition of seemingly contradictory views is not unique to John (as we have just observed), he offers a key to his procedure in his judgment scene of 20:11-15, where he contrasts "books" and the "book of life." People are judged by what they have done; yet, what is ultimately decisive is whether one's name is inscribed in the book of life. John maintains this tension throughout. In consciously paradoxical language and imagery he seeks on the one hand to present human responsibility and on the other hand to portray the finally victorious mercy of a gracious God.

For our purpose, the relevant factor is that a stream, sometimes hidden, yet flowing in steadfast hope, wends through the somber landscape of Revelation. Could it be otherwise for one who had discerned the conquering God in the Lamb who was slain? Now we turn to a selection of the Revelation texts that point toward universal salvation.

Texts Concerning Salvation

1:7   Look! He is coming with the clouds;
every eye will see him,
even those who pierced him; and on his
account all the tribes of the earth will wail.

So it is to be. Amen.

The text is based on a combination of Daniel 7:3 and Zechariah 12:10, a combination which occurs also in Matthew 24:30. When the Judge makes his appearance, he will be manifest to all, even to them whose hostility numbers them with those who had encompassed his death; "all the tribes of the earth" (see 5:9; 7:9; 14:6) does not have the pejorative sense of "the inhabitants of the earth." The "tribes" are, simply, the whole of humankind. "Wail because of him"; does this "wailing" mean despairing lamentation in view of impending condemnation of their former rejection of the Lamb, or contrite lamentation for what they had done to him? In Zechariah 12:10 the context is penitential grief, and this is the better sense here: the tribes of the earth will lament in remorse.

> **5:13** Then I heard every creature in heaven and on earth and under the earth and in the sea, and all that is in them, singing:

> > To the one seated on the throne and to the Lamb
> > be blessing and honor and glory and might forever and ever!

Chapters four and five, closely related, each end on a universal note (4:11; 5:13). "I heard all creatures"; the whole of creation, without exception, joins in the great canticle of praise. John *hears* the chorus of acclamation; to it the four living creatures, heavenly representatives of the created universe, give their "Amen"—and the elders (the heavenly counterpart of the Church) worship. It is universal response: no one and nothing is excluded. The implication is that no part of creation is ultimately rebellious and lost.

> **14:6-7** Then I saw another angel flying in mid-heaven, with an eternal gospel to proclaim to those who live on the earth—to every nation and tribe and language and people. He said in a loud voice, "Fear God and give him glory, for the hour of his judgment has come; and worship him who made

heaven and earth, the sea and the springs of
water.

The angel flies in mid-heaven—the zenith—because
his proclamation is of universal import. "Gospel" (*euan-
gelion*) can only mean "good news." The invitation is
addressed to all of humankind, including "the inhabitants of the earth"—a phrase which, throughout Revelation, designates those who follow the beast (3:10;
11:10; 13:8,12,14; 17:2,8). They are urged to "fear God
and give him glory" (see 11:13)—they are being called
to repentance, to *metanoia* (see Mk 1:14-15). The offer
of repentance and salvation precedes the judgment;
proclamation of the "gospel" heralds the time of salvation.

15:3b-4   Just and true are your ways,
        King of the nations!
    Lord, who will not fear
        and glorify your name?
    For you alone are holy.
        All nations will come
        and worship before you,
    for your judgments have been revealed.

While most manuscripts read "king of the ages," the
better reading is, surely, "king of the nations." The song
holds out hope that the nations, in view of the judgments of the Lord, will fear him and render him homage
and worship. In other words, God is King of the nations,
and the nations will come to acknowledge him as their
King. Our God, even in judgment, is always in the
business of salvation—a God bent on the salvation of
humankind.

20:11-15 Then I saw a great white throne and the one
        who sat on it; the earth and the heaven fled
        from his presence, and no place was found for
        them. And I saw the dead, great and small,
        standing before the throne, and books were

> opened. Also another book was opened, the
> book of life. And the dead were judged according
> to their works, as recorded in the books. And
> the sea gave up the dead that were in it, Death
> and Hades gave up the dead that were in them,
> and all were judged according to what they had
> done. Then Death and Hades were thrown into
> the lake of fire....and anyone whose name was
> not found written in the book of life was thrown
> into the lake of fire.

At the general resurrection, "books" were opened: the books which contain a record of the deeds of the human beings now come for judgment—a common apocalyptic view. The "book of life" is the register of the citizens of the heavenly Jerusalem; it is "the book of life of the Lamb, slain since the foundation of the world" (13:8). "Books were opened...the book of life"; we are faced with the mystery of salvation: people are judged by their deeds, and yet salvation is free gift (v 15). It is gift of a God who manifestly desires the salvation of all (see 1 Tim 2:3-4)—"the living God, who is the Savior of all people" (4:10).

21:3 And I heard a loud voice from the throne saying,

> See, the home of God is among mortals.
> He will dwell with them as their God;
> they will be his peoples...

Again we find a variant reading, "his peoples"; the plural is used instead of the singular "people." John's source is Ezekiel 37:27: "My dwelling place shall be with them; and I will be their God, and they shall be my people." John has extended the prophet's promise to Israel ("people") to all humankind. John utters the promise that God will dwell among his peoples. He was never the God of Israel only; he is not prepared to be the God of Christians only.

43

21:24-27 The nations will walk by its light and the kings of the earth will bring their glory into it. Its gates will never be shut by day—and there will be no night there. People will bring into it the glory and honor of the nations. But nothing unclean will enter it, nor anyone who practices abomination or falsehood, but only those who are written in the Lamb's book of life.

John is manifestly inspired by Isaiah 60. Unlike Isaiah, he is here describing the heavenly Jerusalem. Its inhabitants are not drawn from all nations—they *are* the nations and kings of the earth—thus fulfilling the universalist prophecies of Jewish Scripture. The divine light of the city ("the glory of God gave it light, and its lamp was the Lamb" [v 23]) is a beacon to the nations. These are the "nations" and "kings" that had opposed God's rule and made war on the Lamb and his followers (16:14; 17:18; 18:9; 19:19; 20:8)—the very nations and kings destroyed in the great eschatological battle (19:21; 20:9)! The reference to "nothing unclean" within the city is to be read as a pastoral warning to John's readers. The kingdom of God is not for such as those listed; Christians must seek, here and now, to break with sin.

This has been a selection, no more, but enough, it seems, to have made a point. And the point is that, when one looks more closely at Revelation, beyond the imagery of violence, one finds, firmly expressed, a prospect of universal salvation. One must confess to an uneasiness with the expression "universal salvation." The trouble with the expression is that it might be taken in a manner that trivializes the deadly conflict between good and evil in our history and that cheapens our view of God's mercy and forgiveness. God, not evil, has the last word. God's saving purpose for humankind—the Eschaton, the End—is salvation. There is no negative eschaton: God does not will damnation. For that matter, *positive eschaton only* might be a better way of stating what "universal salvation" is meant to express. Salvation is offered to all. But God is God of freedom; he will not compel. Whether any person, faced with Infinite Love, can choose to embrace evil (and, at some point, the choice must be stark—anything less would be unworthy of our God) we do not know. God and the Lamb alone know what names are inscribed in the book of life.

The apocalyptist seeks to turn his readers from any truck with Evil—and he sees evil embodied in the Roman Empire. The apocalyptic End will come in the total destruction and final disappearance of Evil—in the traditional eschatological battle. The Christian prophet understands that God's final victory has already been won, on the cross. The God who has spoken in the Lamb can only speak his final word in forgiveness and mercy—and salvation. John holds these concerns in tension throughout. It is unfortunate that, in the exuberance of apocalyptic imagery, the first concern has tended to drown out that other word.

For Personal and Group Reflection

1. John wrote to challenge what he thought was rotten in the world of his day. What do you think is rotten in our present world?

2. Other scripture writers did not view things in the same way John did; they did not demonize Rome but suggested dialogue. Give examples of critical issues in today's Church where significant leaders propose different responses. How do these differences affect the faithful?

3. The Pastorals called believers to be "good citizens." Given your Christian

convictions, what do you think it means to be a good citizen today?

4. If the authors of Revelation and the Pastorals were presenting their views today, which one would you follow and why?

5. John saw that sin was institutionalized in the structures of his day. Where do you as a group or parish community see institutionalized sin today, and what if anything do you or should you do to counteract it?

6. If you were to write a "revelation" today, which structures would you prophetically denounce and why?

7. John had a vision of "universal salvation"; do you? Exemplify personal and parish attitudes and practices that show the conviction of universal salvation.

8. John is a prophetic figure in the early Church, challenging people by his writings. How do you live out your responsibility to a prophetic ministry today? What do you stand for? Which aspects of your life prophetically call others to new values?

Chapter Three

The Communities of John's Concern

I t is clear that John knows well the churches he addresses. He is disturbed by attitudes in the churches, notably a willingness to come to terms with the prevailing social environment. He perceives a radical incompatibility between that Roman world and the gospel message. In his dualistic view, the perennial conflict is being played out in terms of Rome and the Church. John's stance is uncompromising; Christians may not, in any measure, be followers of the beast (Rome). His is a minority position. First-century Christians, by and large, had learned to live within the Roman system. John stands as a challenge. He is a reminder, now and then, that the demands of Caesar may be in conflict with the claims of God. He proposes his view with prophetic singlemindedness and apocalyptic exuberance.

If John calls for separation from Rome, he does not call for a break with the existing Christian communities. He is strictly critical of some within the Asian communities—the Nicolaitans, "Jezebel" (2:15,20)— but he does not regard them as outsiders. He seeks to polarize the churches in Asia by claiming that there is only one genuinely Christian attitude toward the contemporary world. He is clear that it is wrong for a Christian to settle for any form of accommodation to that world—because he is convinced that the Roman world is demonic through and through.

An apocalyptic group tends to be sectarian—seeing itself as the true remnant of God's people. Such an attitude does figure in Revelation. John would have stood in opposition to the larger Christian community that had developed a modus vivendi with the contemporary social order. He and his adherents were a "deviant" group that chose to oppose the public order. He and they represent alienation, but alienation of their own choosing. It is a moot point as to what following John had and what support he might have found in the Asian churches. As an itinerant prophet—for such he seems to have been—John could be radical. Could a Christian, in Thyatira, say, with family obligations, afford to be as radical? Yet, the fact of Revelation and the forthright tone of the messages (chapters 2-3) strongly suggest that John did not stand alone.

John could not fail to see that his rejection of Rome, his policy of opposition to everything Roman, must invite a stern reaction from the "demonic" Empire. Any Christian community built along his lines would necessarily be on a collision course with any authority structure built on power. In his perspective, persecution was an inevitable, and imminent, prospect. If Revelation is not to be linked with actual upheaval and crisis, it may be seen as representing an uncompromising minority view. There is its challenge.

The Communities Who Receive John's Challenge

The Messages to the Churches (Chapters 2-3)

To understand John better, it will help to situate him in his Christian world. We need to be circumspect because we see the churches through his eyes only. And he has given us clear enough indication that not all in Asia shared his analysis of the situation. With this proviso, we seek to learn what we can of these communities. Obviously, the messages to the seven churches (chapters 2-3) will be of prime concern.

Revelation is firmly addressed: "John to the seven churches of Asia" (1:4). The churches are named: Ephesus, Smyrna, Pergamum, Thyatira, Sardis, Philadelphia, and Laodicea (1:11). Seven is a symbolic number representing the whole Church of John's area. We know of at least three others besides the churches listed—Troas (2 Cor 2:12), Colossae (Col 1:1) and Hierapolis (Col 4:13). Each church of the chosen seven will hear a verdict based on a precise knowledge of its situation, both external (there are topical references) and spiritual. The churches receive praise or blame (or both), usually with some qualifications, and in this there seems to be a definite plan or progression. Ephesus receives censure and commendation; then, Smyrna, Thyatira, and Philadelphia (the even numbers) are praised, the latter with marked warmth, while Pergamum, Sardis, and Laodicea are censured, the last very severely. The arrangement is somewhat stylized.

John is not addressing an abstract "church." He speaks, directly, to communities of men and women—communities good, bad, and indifferent. The messages peg Revelation firmly to our world. It is word of hope to people who need hope, people who may falter. This realism—and we find it throughout Christian Scripture—brings us comfort and encouragement. There never has been a perfect Christian community. Christians have been faithful and heroic, and Christians have been frail and vacillating. It is not enough for us to find solace in the word to Philadelphia; we must also hearken to the word to Laodicea.

Ephesus

Ephesus, which stood at the mouth of the river Cayster, was the leading city of the Roman province of Asia. It was populous, privileged, and wealthy, the chief port and market city of Asia. Paul had visited the city for the first time toward the close of 51 CE (Acts 18:19-21). He returned for a lengthy stay of about three years (53-58 CE [Acts 19-20]). From there he sent disciples to other cities of Asia.

Because he has seen with eyes "like a flame of fire" (Rev 1:14), the Lord knows the "works"—good (2:2-3,6) and bad (2:4)—of his church. The praiseworthy works of the church are its "toil" in resisting and overcoming false teachers—the Nicolaitans (2:6)—and its "patient endurance," for the sake of Christ, in the labors and trials of the effort (2:3). The Ephesian Christians had not emerged unscathed from their struggle with false teachers (that is, those whom John regarded as such); they had maintained orthodoxy, but their love had waned. Although the loss of their initial love is grievous, the Ephesians still have in their favor that they hate the deeds which Christ also hates (2:6). Did zeal for truth push them too far and prove to be cause of their failure to love? Sadly, later Christian history has too many instances of unholy zeal in pursuit of "truth." Orthodoxy is no substitute for orthopraxis. It surely cannot replace the praxis of love.

"Victor"—one who conquers—appears in all the messages. The victor is one who "continues to do my works to the end" (2:26), one who shared the victory of Christ

(3:21), who won his victory by the laying down of life. This is not to say that John expected all Christians to suffer martyrdom or that he believed that only martyrs shared the blessedness of Christ. Always the purpose of the book must be kept in mind. He writes to encourage his readers in what he perceives to be an hour of imminent peril. Persecution looms and there will be victims; it is a threat that all must face.

Smyrna

Smyrna, modern Izmir, lay thirty-five miles north of Ephesus at the head of a splendid harbor. In Roman times it was one of the most prosperous cities of Asia. In 26 CE, a temple to Tiberius was built there. The city was second only to Pergamum as a center of emperor-cult. The Christians of Smyrna were beset by trials and, in a wealthy city, were materially poor, but they were rich in spiritual goods, in faith (2:9). Christians were in conflict with a strong Jewish element in Smyrna. Jews had special, imperially acknowledged privileges, and Judaism was a *religio licita*, formally recognized by the state. Christians, at first exclusively, or predominantly, Jewish as they were, would have sheltered under the Jewish umbrella. But as the movement became increasingly Gentile and distanced itself from Judaism, Jews might denounce Christians as members of an unauthorized cult. Christians did not help matters by claiming to be the true Israel. Such a claim—by Gentiles!—could not be stomached by ethnic Jews. And, indeed, there is an arrogant ring to characterization of the synagogue as those "who say that they are Jews and are not" (2:9). It is the perennial temptation of a religious group to make exclusive claims.

Pergamum

Pergamum stood forty miles north of Smyrna. In John's time it appears to have been the administrative headquarters of the province of Asia. In 29 BCE, it had a temple dedicated to Rome (the *Dea Roma*) and Augustus, the first of the cities of Asia in which the imperial cult was established. It remained pre-eminently the focus of emperor-cult in the province. The church of Pergamum was in a particularly difficult situation, though the nature of that situation is not entirely clear. Whatever the pressure, the Christians there had stood faithful (23:13). But, while the church had withstood dangers from without, it had dealt less successfully with false doctrine within. The Christians of Pergamum had been remiss in harboring Nicolaitans (Christians whose views differed from those of John). They are bidden to repent—likely, to reject not only the teaching but the teachers as well.

There was external pressure. Devotees of emperor worship looked askance at those "disloyal" and subversive people. One of the community, Antipas, had paid the ultimate price. Whatever the pressure, the Christians have stood fast (2:13). In John's view, betrayal within was far more serious; for him, any compromise with the prevailing culture was betrayal (2:14-15). His was a typically radical prophetic stance which must have looked extreme to those whom he scathingly likens to Balaam (2:14). But, his prophetic word remains a challenge. Cultural adaptation is all very well; too readily, however, Christians may yield over much to contemporary culture and the Christian challenge may be rendered thoroughly respectable. John would not have much time for a "respectable" Christianity.

Thyatira

Thyatira stood in a broad valley, forty miles southeast of Pergamum. It was primarily a trading center, notable for the number of its trade guilds, many with religious affinities. In contrast to Ephesus (2:4), *agapé* ("love") is not only found among the "works" of Thyatira, but heads the list (2:19). The one fault of the Thyatiran church was that it tolerated the presence of that "Jezebel...who calls herself a prophet" (2:20). The livelihood of Christians in Thyatira depended on membership of the trade guilds—with pagan association. Already, in Corinth, Paul had had to deal with the problem of guild-feasts and the purchase of meat that had been offered in pagan temples (1 Cor 8:1-13; 10:20-30). John is forthright: there can be no compromise. Not all Christians shared his view. Certainly, the Nicolaitans and "Jezebel" (2:14,20) saw the situation differently. In point of fact, "Jezebel," at Thyatira, was a prophetic rival to John, with a notable following (2:20-23). At stake was the question of assimilation: To what extent might Christians conform to the prevailing culture for the sake of economic survival or social acceptance? For John, the only answer was: Not at all! Christians who decided otherwise had sold the pass.

In the reaction to the Nicolaitans at Ephesus, Pergamum, and Thyatira, one is strongly reminded of a situation in the Johannine community, reflected in 1 John. There the author is in polemic against "secessionists" who differ from him on theological (more precisely, christological) grounds. He has not a good word for them. Among other things, they are "antichrists" (1 Jn 2:18-19), children of the devil (3:10), brethren of Cain (3:12). Yet, the secessionists are fellow-Christians—as the Nicolaitans of Revelation are John's fellow-Christians. *Odium theologicum* is no more respectable than any other form of hate.

Sardis

About thirty miles southeast of Thyatira lay Sardis, former capital of the Lydian kingdom of Croesus. In Roman times it was, like Ephesus, a commercial city. It had an unusually prominent Jewish community. The Christians of Sardis are either spiritually dead or in spiritual torpor (3:1-2). Life is not quite extinct, but these Christians must come fully awake and carefully tend the spark of life that does remain, lest it should really be extinguished (3:2-3). The lamentable state of the church is displayed in its half-hearted living of the Christian life. "Remember then" (v 3)—the same recommendation as to the Ephesians (2:5); let them look back to the time when they had willingly listened to the preaching of the gospel and had gladly come to believe. Let them cling now to that faith and promptly turn from their neglect.

Philadelphia

Founded in the second century BCE, arguably as a center for the spread of Greek culture, Philadelphia, a prosperous town, stood thirty miles southeast of Sardis. As at Smyrna, a particular problem of Christians at Philadelphia was Jewish hostility. In contrast to the situation in Smyrna, there is promise of the conversion of the Jewish opposition in Philadelphia (3:9). For the first time in these messages, in relation to this little but faithful church, we find explicit mention of Christ's love: "I have loved you" (v 9). Because they keep his word with the steadfastness that is marked by patient endurance, the Philadelphian Christians will reap their reward: they will be kept safe through the "great ordeal" (7:14). It is clear that Jesus will "keep safe" the Philadelphians not only because of their steadfastness but because they are little and weak, and they know it, thus letting Christ work through their weakness (3:8). Even here the paradox is sustained, for safekeeping does not mean exemption from tribulation but efficacious support through it.

Laodicea

Laodicea, forty miles southeast of Philadelphia, in the valley of the Lycus, developed under Roman rule into a major commercial city. The material prosperity of Laodicea is reflected in the attitude of the church which believes itself rich in spiritual possessions and in want of nothing (3:17). The rebuttal is emphatic: You are the wretched one *par excellence*. It is also "poor, blind, and naked"—ironic allusions to the banking, eye-ointment, and clothing industries of Laodicea, objects of its self-complacency (3:17-18). The severity of the rebuke, with its implied threat, is really a sign of Christ's concern, of his love (3:19). He who loves the humble, faithful Philadelphians (3:9) loves also the self-sufficient, lukewarm Laodiceans.

Key Teachings to the Churches

The messages to the churches are vitally important for a proper understanding of Revelation. While John seems to have his eyes fixed on the heavenly world, his feet are, all the while, firmly on the ground. The communities to and for whom he writes are communities of real men and women, of people who are coping, not always effectively, with difficult and painful situations. If the humble and faithful Philadelphians and the Christians of Smyrna earn unstinted praise, the self-sufficient Laodiceans, doubtless to their chagrin and incredulous surprise, hear only words of blame, while the church of Sardis is told that it is more dead than alive. The Ephesians may have sustained orthodoxy— but at the cost of intolerance. On the other hand, the

situation in Thyatira and Pergamum warns that tolerance may be pushed too far.

Assessment and verdict are those of the Lord of the
churches—but filtered through the mind and words of
the prophet. John's own temperament and uncompromising stance have colored his judgment and his
words. Is "that woman Jezebel" quite as black as he
has painted her? Does she, perhaps, propose a way of
Christian living which, though unacceptable to John,
is not really incompatible with the gospel? Are the
Jewish communities in the various cities really "syna-
gogues of Satan" (2:9; 3:9)? Still, if John displays a
measure of intolerance, he has, as we have seen, a
refreshing appreciation of the infinite stretch of God's
mercy.

Church and World

John had turned his back on the Roman way. When
announcing the fall of Babylon (18:2-8) he has a heavenly voice proclaim: "Come out of her, my people, so
that you may not take part in her sins" (18:4). He
describes the end of the city of Rome; the people he
addresses are not in Rome but in the province of Asia.
They "come out" of Rome by resisting and rejecting the
culture and values of the Empire. John's rejection of
Rome and all it stands for is total; he wants his
Christians to be as radical as he. Such being the case,
he has no doubt that *thlipsis*, "tribulation," will be an
essential component of Christian living. It is so even
before the *great* tribulation. Thus, in the message to
Smyrna: "I know your tribulation and your poverty"
(2:9). The response to tribulation is *hypomoné*, "patient
endurance," the staying power of God's people. The
word occurs seven times in Revelation (1:9; 2:2,3,19;
3:10; 13:10; 14:12). This is the characteristic virtue of
the persecuted, of those steadfastly enduring "tribula-

tion." It is founded on faith in Jesus, the Lord who comes, and is inspired by the certainty of his love.

Tribulation

The sealing of God's servants before the plagues of the trumpets (7:3-8) does not symbolize protection *from* tribulation and death but means being sustained in and through tribulation. When the temple of God is measured and so brought under God's special care (11:1), the outer court is left unmeasured, vulnerable (11:2). If the woman of chapter 12 has her "safe house" in the desert (12:6,14) the furious dragon wages war on her offspring (12:17). In other words, while the Church (symbolized by temple and woman) has the assurance of divine preservation, Christians are open to the assault of dragon and beasts. The paradox is that the victims of the assault are the victors—here is the divine protection. The Lamb (1:18; 5:9,12; 12:15; 17:14; 19:13) and his followers (2:10; 7:14-17; 11:11-12; 12:11; 14:4; 20:4-6) conquer by dying!

The dragon conjured up the fearsome beast (Rome), a beast "allowed to wage war on God's people and conquer them" (13:7). John will hold out no fanciful hope of miraculous deliverance. The tribulation is a painful fact of life:

> If you are to be taken captive,
>   into captivity you go;
> if you kill with the sword,
>   with the sword you must be killed.

> Here is a call for the endurance and faith of the saints (13:10).

It is an aside, a special admonition to Christians. The day of persecution is at hand. Christians will be saved through the persecution, not from it. Captivity, exile, death—such may be the fate of the faithful. Again there is summons to *hypomoné*, patient endurance. Christian endurance is a sharing in the passion of Christ; faith perceives there the true victory.

The Victors

In 19:1-6 a great multitude, seemingly that "great multitude" of 7:9-10, sings a victory song. A special cause of rejoicing is that "the marriage of the Lamb has come" (19:7). In Revelation those who form the bride of Christ have been redeemed "by the blood of the Lamb" (5:9; 7:14; 14:3-4). The bride of the Lamb "has made herself ready" (19:7), yet her wedding gown is gift: "it is granted her" to attire herself in fine linen—nothing other than "the righteous deeds of the saints" (19:8). The bride, then, is the Church. Compare Ephesians 5:25-27:

> ...Christ loved the church and gave himself up
> for her, in order to make her holy by cleansing
> her with the washing of water by the word, so as
> to present the church to himself in splendor,
> without a spot or wrinkle or anything of the
> kind—yes, so that she may be holy and without
> blemish.

The Church is no abstraction; it is the community of Christian men and women, followers of the Lamb, made one with him in baptism. And if the adornment of the Church is good deeds, they, too, ultimately, are gift. "What have you that you did not receive?" (1 Cor 4:7).

At the End there will be a new heaven, a new earth, a new Jerusalem (21:1-2). God will come to dwell, definitively, with humankind. And, again, there is comforting assurance.

The victors will have this heritage; "and I will be their God and they will be my children" (21:7). Reference to the "victors" carries the reader back to the messages (chapters 2-3). "Those who conquer will inherit these things" is an eighth promise that embraces and rounds off the former seven promises (2:7,10,17,26-27; 3:5,12,21). One should have in mind the pastoral concern of John. While this is most evident in the prophetic messages of chapters 2-3, John keeps it in sight throughout and it becomes more pronounced in the final chapters. This explains why at 21:8 he takes care to list practices that have no place, nor ever could have, in the Holy City. They characterize the "old self," which those who would enter the city must "put off" (Col 3:5-10). His concern is faithful witness in the present. Since the warning is addressed to Christians, John chooses to deck sin in lurid colors (see 9:20-21). The "liars" (21:8) are all who are opposed to Christ, the faithful and true (3:14; 19:11), and who have been seduced by the dragon, "the deceiver of the whole world" (12:9). Such as they do not share in the heritage of the saints.

Martyrs

The word *martys* ("witness") occurs frequently in Revelation. Once only ("And I saw that the woman was drunk with the blood of the saints and with the blood of the witnesses to Jesus" [17:6]) does the word *martys* carry the precise sense of "martyr." Nonetheless, there is no doubt that John envisaged not only *thlipsis*, "tribulation," but accepted that many faithful Christians would fall victim to the wrath of the beast. In effect, these are "martyrs." The martyrs are those who have come out of the great tribulation; they are clothed in the white of victory for they have washed their robes in the blood of the Lamb (7:13-14). They have conquered Satan by the blood of the Lamb (12:11); they have been victorious over the beast and its image (15:2). Hence, in the messages, "the Victor" is, first and foremost, the "martyr"—one who has won the victory, as Christ has won the victory, by the laying down of life.

This is not to say that John expected all Christians to suffer martyrdom or that he believed that only martyrs share the blessedness of Christ. Always, the purpose of the book must be kept in mind. He writes to encourage his readers in what he perceived to be an hour of imminent peril. Persecution looms and there will be victims; it is a threat that all must face. John does not cloak that grim prospect. He understands that his chilling warning must be cushioned by some measure of comfort—a generous measure, indeed. Accordingly, he takes care to stress the blessedness, beyond death, of the victims of tribulation. A look at the main texts will make the point.

> I saw under the altar the souls of those who had
> been slaughtered for the word of God and for
> the testimony they had given (6:9).

John has in mind Christians who will die in the great persecution that (in his view) is about to break. The striking imagery—"under the altar"—is suggested by Leviticus 4:7: "the rest of the blood...he shall pour out at the base of the altar of burnt offering"; and, since "the life is in the blood" (Lev 17:11), the "souls" of martyrs are where their life-blood is found. Besides, it was current rabbinical belief that the souls of the righteous rested underneath the altar in heaven. Here we have Christian faithful, slain for their fidelity to the one God and for their "testimony" to Jesus by sharing his fate.

> ...the accuser of our comrades has been
> thrown down...
> But they have conquered him by the blood
> of the Lamb
> and by the word of their testimony,

> for they did not cling to life even in the face of
> death (12:10-11).

Satan had been cast out of heaven (12:7-9). The victors rejoice in a heaven free of his baneful presence. Again, the nature of their "testimony" is unmistakable. They are victors because they have mingled their blood with the blood of the Lamb.

Harvest

In 14:1-5 the 144,000 companions of the Lamb are those who were sealed in 7:1-8; they are the victors of the messages. "These have been redeemed from humankind as firstfruits for God and the Lamb" (14:4). Jesus is *the* firstfruit of the dead, of those who belong to him. These redeemed ones are the firstfruits of the harvest of salvation.

> And I heard a voice from heaven saying, "Write
> this: Blessed are the dead who from now on die
> in the Lord." "Yes," says the Spirit, "they will
> rest from their labors, for their deeds follow
> them (14:13).

John's picture of retribution just before the above passage is a pastoral warning to his readers (14:6-12). They may be shaken by persecution or seduced by the glamour of the Empire. He seeks to bring home to them just how terrible would be a turning from the following of Christ. Faithfulness to him is the path of life; any other way is a road to death. Yet, death in faithfulness to him is "rest"—rest that is beginning of new life. The good deeds of their earthly life will win their reward.

> So the one who sat on the cloud swung his
> sickle over the earth, and the earth was reaped
> (14:16).

"One like the Son of Man," the Lamb, waits for the word of the Father (see Mk 13:32). The "son of man" harvests his elect. Compare this with Mark 13:26-27: "Then they will see 'the Son of Man coming in clouds' with great power and glory. Then he will send out the angels, and gather his elect from the four winds...."

Judges

> Then I saw thrones, and those seated on them were given authority to judge. I also saw the souls of those who had been beheaded for their testimony to Jesus and for the word of God....They came to life and reigned with Christ a thousand years....This is the first resurrection. Blessed and holy are those who share in the first resurrection (20:4-6).

In his millennium vision John sees the victors being commissioned as judges of humankind (see Dan 7:22)—as they will be priests and kings (Rev 20:6). They achieve their true status as victors. The standard Jewish view was of a general resurrection of the dead at the End. John is alone in his notion of two resurrections. His "first resurrection" means that "those who have been beheaded" already reign with Christ, he "who was dead and came to life" (2:8). John wants to sustain his stress on the privilege of martyrs; he has to find a way of underlining that privilege. Seen in this light, his concept of a first resurrection makes sense. It is his way of stressing not only the blessedness but the status of the martyrs. Since the martyrs are "firstfruits," they are representative of Christians. It is they, the "blessed and holy," who enjoy the first resurrection.

John's concern for the Christians of Asia is manifest. From his word to them we learn something of these communities. They were certainly a minority in all these Asian towns; they were a small speck in the population of the Empire. Yet, John expects them to challenge the Empire. Their challenge, while wholly non-violent, is to be radical in the extreme: total rejection of Rome. We perceive that, to some at least, this was an unrealistic demand; the messages show that John faced opposition. We have no way of knowing the strength of his following. But there surely were those who shared his view—this is evident from the tone of the work. He has no doubt that he holds out a grim prospect. His insistent and repeated emphasis on the blessedness of "martyrs" is revealing: those who will hearken to his word need every encouragement he can offer.

Things did not work out quite as John had envisaged. The beast was not destroyed as promptly as he had hoped. We still await the New Jerusalem. Nevertheless, we owe a debt to John and his adherents. We are reminded that if Jesus ruled, "Give to Caesar the things that are Caesar's, and to God the things that are God's" (Mk 12:17), he insisted, too, that the claims of God are all-embracing (12:29-30). Christians could deduce from Jesus' principle that Christianity need involve no disloyalty to the state. But principle it remained, and they had to work out for themselves the implication of it. It is not always easy to draw a clear line between a civil sphere where Caesar has his rights and a religious sphere where God rules. It is not always easy to discern what rightfully belongs to Caesar and where loyalty to the state makes unacceptable demands. John's uncompromising stance does, painfully, remind us that a situation can arise where the decision has to be, or ought to be, *Non serviam!*: "I will not obey!" Such situations have arisen, and in this century. We can always find ways of evading the challenge of such as John.

For Personal and Group Reflection

1. John is disturbed by the attitudes of some Christian communities in his day but never breaks with them. How does

this challenge us in our approaches to other Christian groups, both within and outside our own tradition?

2. John claims that his view is the only correct one. Do you think he was right? Do you think he is still right?

3. John was probably viewed as encouraging sectarian communities that opposed public order. Can you think of present-day examples of such approaches? What do you think of such groups today? What do you think John's contemporaries thought of him and his communities?

4. The Ephesian community is praised and challenged, but most significantly is criticized because the prophet says, "[Y]ou have abandoned the love you had at first" (Rev 2:4). Has your love and enthusiasm for Christ grown cold?

5. The community in Smyrna is urged, "Do not fear what you are about to suffer....[S]o that you may be tested... you will have affliction. Be faithful... (Rev 2:10). What are the trials you must face as Christians today, individually and as communities?

6. The church of Pergamum seemed to have accommodated unacceptable views internal to the community. Are there any positions accepted by local Christians seeking to adapt to local culture that are unacceptable to the fundamentals of the faith?

7. John condemns other Christian leaders who hold different views than he. Was he right, or was he just arrogant about his own religious views? Are there any similar situations today?

8. John condemns Sardis for its mediocrity. "Wake up, and strengthen what remains and is on the point of death, for I have not found your works perfect in the sight of my God" (Rev 3:2). Mediocrity is a constant temptation for most believers. Is this a suitable challenge for you, individually and as a parish community?

9. To the Philadelphian community the seer states: "Look, I have set before you an open door, which no one is able to shut" (Rev 3:8). The Vatican Council II was such an open door, but it takes much courage to walk through an open door. Have you, your family, and the parish responded to the great renewal opportunities of recent years?

10. The Laodicean community thinks it does not need to change or renew itself, and yet John criticizes its lukewarmness in religious commitment. What would John's reactions be for each of us and the communities to which we belong?

Chapter Four

God and Lamb

The revelation of Jesus Christ, which God gave him..." (Rev 1:1). John's title firmly describes his work as a revelation from Jesus Christ, with God as the ultimate source. It is a revelation which, at the close, will be attested by Christ himself (22:6). The Almighty God has a plan and a purpose for his world; it will unfold through the mediation of the Lamb (chapter 5). At the end, that purpose accomplished, God and Lamb will dwell among their people (22:3-4). A look at God and Lamb throughout Revelation will give us not only an insight into John's theology and christology but will help us further to understand his work.

God

In Revelation 4:1 John is rapt to heaven. The first object that catches his eye is a throne. He perceives the mysterious presence of One seated on the throne. That One dominates Revelation. The *throne* is the symbol of his almighty power. He is Creator and King of creation. He is the Creator who has total respect for his creation. And creation, in its fashion, unceasingly sings his praise. Yet, all is not well in his world—more particularly in his privileged world of humankind. He had, with calm deliberation, endowed humankind with freedom. He would honor human freedom with divine respect. He, sadly, acknowledged that "the inclination of the human heart is evil from youth" (Gen 8:21). In John's perspective, humankind is set on a path of self-destruction. Evil is rampant in God's world. He is wholly sure that Evil can never have the last word. God will act. He has acted. He had unsheathed the one weapon that would destroy Evil—that had overcome Evil—the cross.

We know God through human perception of God. That perception will always be culturally conditioned; it will be colored by the human and historical situation—by circumstances. As a Christian, John saw his God revealed in the Lamb—the Lamb who was slain. That truth colored his vision of the One on the throne. He would not seek to describe that God, so far beyond any conception of human majesty. Yet, this was no aloof God. He was the God present in the Son. John had been loosed from sin in the blood of that Son (Rev 1:5); he had experienced the love of God. Never, for him, could God be a distant God. This awareness, indeed, was not something wholly new. As a Jew, sensitive to the prophetic tradition, he had been familiar with the reality of a transcendent God immersed in the life of his people. The Christ—presence of God—who walks among John's churches (chapters 2-3) is playing the role that Yahweh had played through his prophets.

"The revelation of Jesus Christ, which God gave him…" (Rev 1:1). God is the ultimate source of revelation. John bears witness to the secret purpose of God of which Jesus Christ is the prime witness. "'I am the Alpha and the Omega,' says the Lord God, who is and who was and who is to come, the Almighty" (1:8). It is the first of only two passages in Revelation where God is explicitly identified as speaker (see 21:5-8). God is

"Almighty," John's favorite title for God. If he is the Almighty, the eternal, sovereign Lord, his might is present in the Lamb (1:4-6). He is ever the foolish God who displays divine power in the cross of Jesus. John's address is full of comfort. We are assured that our God is the everlasting, the Almighty. But we Christians meet this awesome God in the one who laid down his life for us.

The phrase "one seated on the throne" (4:2) occurs twelve times in Revelation. If God may not be seen or described, there is no veiling the majesty of the One on the throne. The tone is set at the heavenly vision of chapter 4, with its hymn to the Lord God Almighty, the *Creator* (4:11). This is echoed in the victory song of 7:9-17, the praise of 11:15-19, the song of Moses and of the Lamb in 15:3-4. In these instances, the *Redeemer* is being acknowledged. Divine sovereignty is manifest in another manner in the judgment of Rome (14:8; 18:1-9; 19:1-10). Through his favorite designation of God—the One seated on the throne—John is making a political statement: Here, and not in Rome, is where *real* authority is to be found. The arrogant throne of Caesar is no match for the throne—a throne that, at the last judgment, becomes the great white throne (20:11). God is all in all.

The "Wrath" of God

If the sovereignty of God is not in question, the exercise of that sovereignty does raise questions. There is, on the face of it, an unsavory side to the wielding of divine power. One might expect violence from the dragon; and there is the prospect of persecution of God's people. Violence comes, principally, from the One on the throne—and from the Lamb! The "wrath" of God is emphasized, a wrath poured out in a series of increasingly destructive plagues. There is a vindictiveness, which is underlined at the close of the vintage scene (14:17-20), with its vision of the "great winepress of God's wrath" and its river of human blood two hundred miles in spate. There is, again, the gruesome feast prepared for birds of prey (19:17-18) in a battle generalled by the Lamb! The Lamb—that should give us pause. John has told us that the Lamb is he who reveals God. Can our God, then, be a God of wrath?

God is the patient God, but he cannot ignore evil; he will not condone oppression. There is a place for his "wrath," his radical incompatibility with evil. He copes with evil in *his* way. His answer to the worst that humankind can perpetrate is the answer of the cross. The great river of blood from the winepress of his wrath (14:19-20) is a warning that innocent blood cannot be shed with impunity. God is not vindictive. God does not punish. The problem for humans—and it is a humanly insoluble problem—is to maintain faith in the long-suffering of God, faith in the infinitely forgiving love of God, and, at the same time, to grasp, and find some way to express, his abhorrence of evil and sin. Our human imagery and our human language are inadequate. Unhappily, we too readily end up presenting an unsavory image of our gracious God.

All the violent action in Revelation wrought on the side of good is wrought by God and the Lamb. Indeed, it is all traced back to the Lamb. The breaking of the first seal (6:1) launched not only the first series of plagues but the other two as well—they are interconnected. As rider on the white horse, the Lamb launches the final, decisive battle (19:11-21).

In 10:1-11, the vision of the open scroll, John receives a fresh prophetic investiture. There is an enigmatic reference to the "seven thunders" (10:3): "When the seven thunders had spoken, I was about to write, but I heard a voice from heaven saying: 'Seal up what the seven thunders have said; do not write it down'" (10:4). The "seven thunders"—the voice of God—might be understood to speak a message of doom; the command to "seal up" means that God has canceled the doom of which the thunders were the symbol. Humanity must be stopped forthwith from endlessly producing the means of its own torment and destruction. The command to John, "Seal up what the seven thunders have said," may be akin to the divine declaration after the flood: "I will never again curse the ground because of humankind...nor will I ever again destroy every living creature as I have done" (Gen 8:21). In the flood story we see the holy God's grief over human sin—"it grieved him to his heart" (6:6). On the other hand, he has decided to put up with humankind's tendency to evil: "for the inclination of the human heart is evil from youth" (8:21). His forebearance will wear down that resistance to his love.

It Was Allowed

When one looks at the plagues, one observes a recurring note, struck in the repetition of the verb *edothé* (literally, "it was given, granted"). The four horsemen are "permitted" to wreak their havoc (6:1-8). A star fallen from heaven was "given" the key of the abyss in order to release the demonic locusts which were "given" destructive powers and were "told" and permitted to torment humankind (9:1-5). The false prophet was "allowed" to bring people to worship the beast, to cause those who refused to do so to be killed, and to compel all to wear the mark of the beast (13:15-16). The role of the "ten horns"—ten kings—of the scarlet beast is especially noteworthy: "For God has put it into their minds to carry out his purpose," that is, the destruction of Rome (17:16-17). Finally, the dragon itself was not only seized and imprisoned and again let loose (20:1-3), but it was let loose only to muster the nations for their—and his—final destruction (20:7-10). John's view is dualistic—a universe divided, in conflict, between good and evil. But there is never any doubt of the outcome. Evil, even in its most potent guise, is subject to the sovereign power of good—the One seated on the throne.

Judgment

At the final judgment scene (20:11-15), John sees "a great white throne." The One seated on the throne has dominated Revelation. He is invisibly, but vibrantly, present in the Lamb. Now is the moment for his final word. The old earth and heaven fade away for ever. Now is the time for the "new heavens and a new earth, where righteousness is at home" (2 Pet 3:13). In the new world of God righteousness reigns not only supreme but wholly. There is no place for any shadow of evil.

The dead, "great and small"—*all* the dead—stand before the throne of judgment. It is judgment, and "books were opened": the books which contain a record of the deeds of human beings now come for judgment. But there is "another book": this book of life is the register of the citizens of the heavenly Jerusalem; it is the book of life of the Lamb. "Books were opened...the book of life": we are faced with the mystery of salvation. People are judged by their deeds; and yet salvation is free gift (v 15). God's choice is not arbitrary and John had warned that a name might be canceled from the book (3:5).

Our God has created us as free beings. He respects our freedom totally; that is why his grace is, so often, thoroughly disguised. We come, later, to discern, in our most painful episodes, his graciousness. Freedom is costly; it exacts the price of responsibility. We are answerable for our deeds — and our omissions. Yet, all the while, our salvation is wholly grace. "Whoever does not receive the kingdom of God as a little child will never enter it" (Mk 10:15). "Justified by his grace as a gift, through the redemption that is in Christ Jesus" (Rom 3:24). We are responsible for what we do; we are judged by works. God is author of our salvation; we are saved by grace. John, like the bible in general, does not attempt to resolve the tension. Later Christian theologians, courageously, stubbornly—and vainly—strove to find a way past the dilemma. The theologians of the Bible, in their wisdom, were content to leave the matter in the hands of God.

New Creation

> Then I saw a new heaven and a new earth; for the first heaven and the first earth had passed away... (21:1).

John has not dragged in his concept of "a new heaven and a new earth." Not alone is the idea thoroughly biblical, but his "new world" opens up the perspective of an eschatological future in which the cosmos is redeemed and perfected. This is not a restoration of our broken world to its imagined original state, but a transformation beyond imagining, a transformation so radical as to be a "new creation." In all of this the human aspect is firmly in mind. Thus, in this new world "death will be no more; mourning and crying and pain will be no more" (21:4). Paul had already spoken of the redemption of the cosmos in the context of human redemption: the whole of nature shares in the birthpangs which lead to the freedom of the children of God (Rom 8:18-23). The biblical view of the world maintains an intimate link between the cosmos and humankind (Gen 1-2).

This is a matter of first importance. It means that the promise of a new world implies a radical questioning of our present relationship with the world—this world as it was originally envisaged by God. It is a reminder that we humans have sinned grievously against God's earth committed to our responsible care (Gen 1:26-30). We are summoned to *metanoia*, called to work toward the new world held in prospect. True, it is God who declares, "I make all things new." But God has freely, from the start, involved humankind in his creation. In his plan a new world for humankind can only be with human involvement.

Life With God

"See, the home of God is among mortals" (21:3). What is eternal life with God? We, in our earthly existence, creatures of time and space, must, perforce, picture heavenly reality in terms of time and space. Here, John has two central images. There will be a new heaven and a new earth. The dragon once had his place in the old heaven; he had ravaged the old earth. A creation that is, at last, utterly free of evil, can only be *new*. Humankind was the summit of God's creation, divine pride and joy (Gen 1:26-31). God's destined home for humankind was the garden of delights (2:15). There will be a new home for humankind in the new creation: a *city*, city of God, the new Jerusalem. It is a heavenly city, yet a habitat of men and women. There the victors find their promised rest.

John surpasses himself in his surrealistic painting of the New Jerusalem. After all, how is one to describe a city of God, a city that is the perfect home of wholly redeemed humankind? It is a city without a temple. God and Lamb reign indeed, but not in the formality of a cultic setting. They dwell in the midst of their people. Our God is never an aloof, distant God—though we tend to make him such. He wants to be with us now. He will be with us always: "He will dwell among them and they will be his peoples" (21:3).

The Lamb

The emergence of the Lamb is dramatic even in the setting of this dramatic book. In his vision of the heavenly throne-room (chapter 5), John had been bidden to look for the Lion of the tribe of Judah. What met his gaze was "a Lamb standing as if it had been slaughtered" (5:5-6). We need not be taken by surprise. After all, John's first characterization of Jesus Christ is as the one "who loves us and freed us from our sins by his blood" (1:5). Indeed, these words are now caught up in the heavenly canticle: "...for you were slaughtered and by your blood you ransomed for God" people from every nation (5:9). "Lamb" is John's favorite title for Christ throughout. We may never overlook that, from the outset, he is the Lamb *who was slain.* If John proceeds to paint the power and triumph of the Lamb, he is clear, and wants it understood, that the decisive victory of the Lamb was won on the cross.

The Faithful Witness

In Revelation 1:5 the three titles of Jesus Christ—"the faithful witness, the firstborn of the dead, and the ruler of the kings of earth"—address directly the situation of John's readers. Jesus stood as faithful witness before Roman authority—a model for Christians in a similar situation. His resurrection as the "first fruits" of general resurrection (see 1 Cor 15:20; Col 1:18) holds out hope to Christians challenged to bear witness unto death. He is God's answer to Caesar's arrogance; he, not Caesar, is universal ruler. This Christ "loves us and has freed us from our sins" (Rev 1:5); he freed us by his death and loves us eternally. Furthermore, he "made us to be a kingdom, priests" (1:6); Christ has constituted his people as a royal house, sharing his authority, and as priestly mediators in the world of humankind. The "us" ("made us") is, obviously, inclusive. Christian women share the royal and priestly role as fully as their brothers.

In Human Form

At Patmos, on the Lord's day, John had a vision of "one in human form" (literally, "one like a son of man"), a human figure dressed in priestly robes. He walks among the "lamps" (the churches); the heavenly Christ is no absentee landlord. He is present in his earthly communities; he knows their "works." It is in his name that John speaks his prophetic messages (chapters 2-3). What is said of the Ancient of Days (God) in Daniel (Dan 7:9) is here said of the one in human form. John, throughout, does not hesitate to use God-language of Jesus. The Christ holds in his right hand (in his power) the seven stars which are the "angels," the heavenly counterparts, of the seven churches. His only weapon is the sword of his mouth (1:16; see 19:21)—the word.

The overall effect of the vision is one of terrifying majesty; John's reaction is that of Daniel (Dan 10:8-9). Yet, this majestic figure remains the Jesus of the Gospel, and John hears again his comforting, "Do not be afraid" (see Mk 6:50; Mt 28:10). John's vision of the risen Lord is dramatic counterpart of the closing declaration of Matthew's Lord: "Remember, I am with you always, to the end of the age" (Mt 28:20). We also have the comfort of his presence in our midst—comfort, but challenge too, as the messages to the churches will underline. We acknowledge this challenge as we worship him as our Lord. But never should we fear in his presence. He is the one who lifts from us even the deep-rooted fear of death, for he, the Living One, is Victor over Death.

The title "Lamb" is not used of Christ in chapters 2-3, but he is that heavenly scrutineer. As "one in human form," he is seen in striking majesty—he is *the* Victor. John falls, in lifeless awe, at his feet, to hear the reassuring voice of the Jesus of the gospel: "Do not be afraid." John realizes that here is no stranger. He walks among his churches. His message to each community is incisive and decisive. He looks at the state of each. He finds love, faithfulness even to death, and patient endurance in face of intolerance and persecution. And he finds failure in love, a willingness to compromise with an inimical world, and the danger of betrayal. Always there is glowing promise to the victors, those who hold steadfast to the end.

Even the stern rebuke (3:15-19) to the Christians of Laodicea, with its implied threat, is really a sign of Christ's concern, of his love (v 19). The gracious words, following hard on the harsh indictment, ring so true: "I am standing at the door, knocking; if you hear my voice and open the door, I will come in to you and eat with you, and you with me" (3:20). Whether praise or blame, there is manifest pastoral concern. The flaming eyes of the Lamb see with the penetrating gaze of a caring God.

The Lamb and the Scroll

When, in chapter 5, John turns to the One on the throne, he sees a scroll lying on the open palm of his right hand. This scroll is God's preordained plan for his world. The opening of the scroll will mean both the revealing of God's purposes and the accomplishing of them. The scroll is sealed. The breaking of the seals is a special, indeed an exclusive, task which the Lamb alone can perform. If John "wept bitterly" (5:4) it is because, as it seems, there is no human agent to set God's purpose for humankind in train. John would have understood that God will not dispense with an agent, such is his respect for humankind. But there is no agent in sight!

One of the elders comforts John by assuring him that all is well. "Then one of the elders said to me, '...the Lion of the tribe of Judah...has conquered....' Then I saw...a Lamb standing as if it had been slaughtered" (5:5-6). In his vision John looked for the emergence of a Lion—and saw a slaughtered Lamb! What he learned, and what he tells his readers, is that the Lion *is* the Lamb: the ultimate power of God ("lion") is manifest on the cross ("lamb"). This is why "Lamb" is John's definitive name for Christ. The Lamb, who enjoys fullness of power and knowledge (5:6), had won the right to break the seven seals. He went to the throne to receive the scroll; receiving the scroll is a transfer of power (5:7).

The mighty Lamb then receives the worship of the living creatures and the twenty-four elders—whom we formerly heard praising God (4:8-10). They sang "a new song" (5:9-10), a song for a great occasion. Here the occasion of the new song is the redemption wrought by Christ. The Lamb is worthy to be God's agent because he was slain—he laid down his life; because he has purchased for God, at the cost of his blood, men and women of every tribe, tongue, people, and nation; because he has made them a royal house of priests.

The Almighty God has a plan and purpose for the world. Our Almighty God manifests power on the cross. In the cross, through the blood of the Lamb, God offers forgiveness and holds out salvation to all. The Lamb, as the manifestation, as the very presence, of our gracious God, is worthy of our honor and worship. He is worthy precisely as the slain Lamb, as the crucified One. Like Paul and Mark, John too in his manner, proposes a *theologia crucis*, a theology of the cross. That comforting—if challenging—theme runs through his work.

The Harvest

In Mark 13:26-27 the Son of man comes "in clouds" to "gather his elect," to harvest them. In Revelation 14:14-20 the "one like the Son of Man" waits for the word of God, who alone knows the hour of judgment (see Mk 13:32). For the faithful ones, that coming will be joy. The harvest is ripe; the wheat is gathered into the heavenly barn. Here, and throughout, in relation to his own, the Lamb displays all the graciousness of God. He has liberated us from the evil deeds of our past. He has purchased from slavery, for God, at the cost of his blood, men and women of every nation, making of them a royal house of priests (Rev 5:9). The victors who have come through the great tribulation have won their victory in virtue of his victory—they have washed their robes in the blood of the Lamb (7:14). He is the Shepherd who will guide them to the water of life (7:17). The victors share in the victory of the Lamb over the dragon; they have conquered him by the blood of the Lamb (12:10-11). They are the faithful ones, marked with the names of the Lamb and of his Father (14:1-5), who "follow the Lamb wherever he goes" (14:4).

As firstfruits of the harvest of the world, the faithful ones represent the whole Church, all those ransomed from the earth. They are those who have been fondly harvested by the one "like a son of man"—the gracious Lamb (14:14-16). The companions of the Lamb are the "armies of heaven" who accompany him, now as invincible rider on the white horse, as he rides out to final victory (19:11-21). John may be pushing the fourth evangelist's triumphal portrayal of the passion and death of Jesus to the limit of apocalyptic imagery. There is the lovelier image of the marriage of the Lamb. The victors are invited to his marriage supper. In the exuberance of John's imagery, guests and Bride are one and the same! (19:7-9). It is the consummation of the Lamb's—and so of God's—love affair with humankind. The imagery first put forward in Hosea 1-3—that of Yahweh as loving spouse of Israel—now, in Revelation, comes to full flowering. Truly, "the home of God is among mortals" (Rev 21:3).

King of Kings

The passage 19:11-21 deals with the victory of Christ and his followers over the beast, the false prophet, and the kings of the earth. It is the great battle of Armageddon (16:16). John sees heaven thrown wide open (19:11) for the parousia of the "one in human form" (1:13). He comes forth majestically, riding a white horse of invincible victory. His very name—Faithful and True—declares him to be upholder of righteousness and integrity. He comes as judge, but his righteousness is vindication of the poor and the meek of the earth (Isa 11:4). He comes as warrior, but his war will be against the destroyers of the earth—the dragon and the beasts. None can escape his scrutiny; all are subject to his authority. He bears a mysterious name (v 12) distinct from the name of verse 13—Word of God—and the titles of verse 16—King of kings and Lord of lords. John, ardent follower of the Lamb, knows that, ultimately, the Lamb is as wondrously mysterious as the gracious God he images.

The rider wears a cloak "dipped in blood." There can be little doubt that John has in mind Isaiah 63:1-3:

> Who is this that comes from Edom,
>   from Bozrah in garments stained
>   crimson?...
>
> Why are your robes red,
>   and your garments like theirs who tread
>   the winepress?
>
> I have trodden the winepress alone,
>   and from the peoples no one was with me;
> I trod them in my anger
>   and trampled them in my wrath;
> their juice spattered on my garments,
>   and stained all my robes.

This is Third Isaiah's violent portrayal of God's victory over Edom—over every enemy of his purpose for Israel. If the rider of Revelation wears a robe dipped in blood as he rides out to join battle, that is because John chooses to portray him in the language of Isaiah. But, then, to be heavily blood-stained *before* battle is distinctly curious. Is John teasing us, challenging us to look more closely at his message? For, if the Lion is the Lamb, if the Victim is the Victor, if to conquer is "to love not one's life even unto death," if there is the intriguing suggestion of universal salvation, then might not John, in a startling rebirth of images, be challenging his readers to reinterpret the imagery to which he and they are heirs? John has reversed the image of Isaiah. He has reversed the image of an avenger splattered with the blood of his enemies. The Lamb is the one who has been pierced (Rev 1:7).

The Lamb goes out, conquering and to conquer; his weapon is the word of his mouth. In this "war" there is no battle; the two beasts are captured without a blow being struck. The armies of heaven are passive spectators; they take no part in the action. Any "slaying" is done by the rider alone, wielding that sword "which came out of his mouth." As Michael's victory over the dragon was really victory of the Lamb (12:11), so, here, victory over the beasts is his victory alone. It is, throughout, John's position that the only battle, the decisive battle, fought by the Lamb was on the cross. There is the Christian victory. Christian victors conquer by the blood of the Lamb and in no other way.

Come, Lord Jesus!

"See, I am coming soon; my reward is with me..." (22:12). It surely is Christ who speaks. His coming is a blessing for the one who has hearkened to the challenging and encouraging prophetic message of John. Inspired by the Spirit, the Church ("the bride") prays its *marana tha,* "Our Lord, Come!" The Church (the earthly Church) responds with eager joy to the Lord's announcement of his coming. The prayer is to be caught up by every hearer of the book (see 1:3); the

Lord looks for the response of the individual Christian
(see 3:20-21). For the Church is no vague personifica-
tion; it is a living organism of living men and women.

Christ, who gives his own solemn testimony to the
contents of the book, assures his Church that he is
coming soon. It is a response to the earnest prayer of
the Church, "Come!" (v 17), and a link with the promise
at the start of the book: "Look! He is coming with the
clouds" (1:7). But this time the promise stands in the
liturgical context of the Eucharist. To the divine assurance "Yes" corresponds the human response "Amen"
(22:20), expressing the absolute faith in his word of the
seer and those whom he represents. John closes with
the prayer that conveys all the longing of his belea-
guered communities: "Come, Lord Jesus."

God and Lamb

A distinctive feature of John's presentation of the
Lamb is his assimilation of the Lamb to God. It is his
way of presenting God as the God who has revealed
himself in Jesus Christ, who has defined himself in
Christ. This conjunction of God and Lamb, as in 5:13—
"To the one seated on the throne and to the Lamb / be
blessing and honor and glory and might / forever and
ever"—which recurs in 7:10; 21:22; 22:1,3, represents
an advanced christology. The same worship is offered
to God and Lamb, just as the throne of both is the same.
The multitude of the saved attribute their victory to
"God and the Lamb" (7:10). The heavenly Jerusalem
has no temple—"its temple is the Lord God the Almighty and the Lamb"—and the Lamb is the lamp of
the heavenly city (21:22-23). When the throne appears
for the last time, now in the city-temple, it is "the throne
of God and of the Lamb" (22:1,3). Throughout 22:3-4
the pronoun "his" (his servants, his face, his name)
refers to God and Lamb in tandem. Accordingly, the

Lamb can declare of himself: "I am the Alpha and the Omega, the first and the last, the beginning and the end" (22:13)—echoing the words of the One on the throne (21:6). We might understand the Lamb to speak as does the Johannine Jesus: "I and the Father are one" (Jn 10:30).

The parallel is instructive. The Johannine Jesus is one with the Father precisely because he is the one sent, the agent of the Father, and is thereby empowered to speak the words of God. John's Lamb is the "faithful witness" (Rev 1:5) who has received his revelation from God (Rev 1:1). It is because of his faithfulness to his witness-bearing, a faithfulness that brought him to the cross, that he shares the throne of God. It is no less clear to the Lamb than it is to the Johannine Jesus that "the Father is greater than I" (Jn 14:28); the one sent and the faithful witness have this in common. They also share the declaration: "Whoever has seen me has seen the Father" (Jn 14:9). "I and the Father are one..."; "the throne of God and of the Lamb"—these tell us nothing of the "nature" of the Son/Lamb but tell us everything of the role of Revealer that is the role of the Son/Lamb. For each John, Jesus is the one in whom God is fully present. God is the one who reveals himself wholly in Jesus.

For Personal and Group Reflection

1. Images of God change according to generations and cultures. John uses "Lamb." What are the most significant images of God for you and for the contemporary Church?

2. Sometimes religion has the unsavory dimension of violence associated with it—the wielding of divine power, the violence of the Lamb, the seeming vindictiveness of the wrath of God, the

image of crucifixion. With which aspects are you uncomfortable and why? How do you cope with them?

3. The Lamb launches the plagues as God launched them in the Jewish scriptures. How do you explain to yourself and to others this involvement of God in humankind's history—this great river of blood from the winepress of God's wrath (Rev 14:19-20)?

4. How should a Christian view the final judgment? Should he or she fear it or look forward to it? What does John say about this?

5. God involves humankind in the ongoing work of creation. It is a conversion to work toward a new creation of the world. What are some of the ecological implications of such a vision?

6. John's portrait of Jesus focuses on the Lamb, who is always present to the churches. How do you experience Jesus' continual presence, individually, in your family, in your local parish community?

7. Like other writers of the Christian scriptures, John presents Jesus as the slain Lamb, the crucified One. What place does this theology of the cross play in your life?

8. The marriage of the Lamb is the consummation of God's love affair with humankind. How do you experience this love in your own life?

9. "See, I am coming soon; my reward is with me, to repay according to everyone's work" (Rev 22:12). Do you want Jesus to come soon? Why or why not? In what way do you wish him to come soon to you?

10. What does the writer of Revelation add to your image of God?

Chapter Five

Liturgy and the Book of Revelation

Revelation is explicitly designated for public reading in a liturgy (1:3), most likely a eucharistic liturgy. From the heavenly celebration that meets John's eyes and ears in chapter 4, there follows, throughout his book, one heavenly liturgy after another. Worship unites heaven and earth. In Revelation the object of worship is the One on the throne—and the Lamb. Every creature "in heaven and on earth and under the earth and in the sea" sings praise (5:13); the souls of the martyred dead cry out (6:9-10); the prayers of God's people are presented to the Lamb (5:8). Worship breaks down all boundaries. In worship all are equal. Worship establishes what is true, what is real. It is a response to the admonition of the Lord: "Strive *first* for the kingdom of God and his righteousness..." (Mt 6:33).

Not only by its liturgical setting but also through an insistent liturgical emphasis throughout, Revelation makes its statement on the centrality of worship in Christian life. So central, indeed, is worship that the inimical "inhabitants of the earth" are also intent on worship—they are worshipers of the beast (13:4). John is making the thoroughly biblical point: Human creatures are, as creatures, subject to some lordship. One must serve God—or Mammon, whatever shape Mammon may assume. The choice is of fundamental importance. John is sure that idolatry corrupts the created order. Worship of God and the Lamb prepares for and hastens the coming of the new heaven and new earth where righteousness dwells.

John does not treat, explicitly, of liturgy in the earthly churches. His concern is the archetypal liturgy of heaven. In his description of heavenly liturgies he is, undoubtedly, influenced by his knowledge of—it may be, past experience of—the worship of Israel. His many hymns are doubtless modeled on, or they reflect, early Christian hymns. Here, we look at these liturgical passages.

Key Liturgical Passages

4:8-11

8 Day and night without ceasing they sing:

"Holy, holy, holy,
the Lord God the Almighty,
who was and is and is to come!"

9 And whenever the living creatures give glory and honor and thanks to the one who is seated on the throne, who lives forever and ever...

10 ...the twenty-four elders fall before the one who is seated on the throne and worship the one who lives forever and ever; they cast their crowns before the throne, singing:

11 "You are worthy, our Lord and God,
to receive glory and honor and power,

for you created all things,
>   and by your will they existed and were
>   created!

John, introduced to heaven (4:1), had a vision of a throne and One seated on it: the Lord God Almighty. The "twenty-four elders" about the throne (4:4) are kings, seated on thrones and wearing crowns. Throughout Revelation they have a cultic role (4:9-10; 5:8-11; 11:16-18; 19:4). They fittingly represent the people of God, that "royal house of priests" (1:6). They are the heavenly counterpart of the earthly Church. The "four living creatures" (4:6) symbolize the created cosmos. The canticle of verse 8, based on Isaiah 6:3, is the unceasing song of nature in praise of its Creator. Human minds and tongues give shape and voice to that praise of animal and inanimate creation (vv 10-11). The Creator is worthy of all honor; he deserves to be worshiped in our earthly liturgy. This vision might inspire us to more fitting celebration.

5:8-14

8 When he had taken the scroll, the four living creatures and the twenty-four elders fell before the Lamb, each holding a harp and golden bowls full of incense, which are the prayers of the saints.

9 They sing a new song:

> "You are worthy to take the scroll
>   and to open its seals,
> for you were slaughtered and by your blood
>   you ransomed for God
>   saints from every tribe and language and
>   people and nation;

10   you have made them to be a kingdom and
>   priests serving our God,
>   and they will reign on earth."

11 Then I looked, and I heard the voice of many
angels surrounding the throne and the living
creatures and the elders; they numbered
myriads of myriads and thousands of thousands,

12 singing with full voice:

> "Worthy is the Lamb that was slaughtered
> to receive power and wealth and wisdom and
> might
> and honor and glory and blessing!"

13 Then I heard every creature in heaven and on
earth and under the earth and in the sea, and
all that is in them, singing:

> "To the one seated on the throne and to the
> Lamb
> be blessing and honor and glory and might
> forever and ever!"

14 And the four living creatures said, "Amen!" And
the elders fell down and worshiped.

The living creatures and the twenty-four elders
whom we had heard worship God (4:8-10) here worship
the Lamb. In keeping with their cultic function, the
elders hold harps and censers; they exercise the
priestly office of mediation, offering the prayers of the
faithful to God. Their "new song" celebrates the redemption wrought by Christ. The Lamb is worthy to be
God's agent because he was slain—had laid down his
life; because he has purchased for God, at the cost of
his blood, men and women of every tribe, tongue,
people, and nation; because he has made them a royal
house of priests. This time a countless host of angels
joins in the heavenly praise. The doxology addressed to
the Lamb (v 12) is more fulsome than that earlier
addressed to the Creator (4:11). Finally, the whole of
creation, without exception, joins in the great canticle
(v 13). John *hears* the sound of the great acclamation;

to it the four living creatures, heavenly representatives of the created universe, give their "Amen"—and the elders worship as in 4:9-10. We may observe that, regularly, eschatological drama arises in a liturgical setting and often climaxes in heavenly worship and liturgical acclamations. This is so of the series of plagues: seals (5:8-14; 7:9-12), trumpets (8:3-4; 11:15-19), bowls (15:2-4).

7:9-12

9 After this I looked, and there was a great multitude that no one could count, from every nation, from all tribes and peoples and languages, standing before the throne and the Lamb, robed in white, with palm branches in their hands.

10 They cried out in a loud voice, saying,

"Salvation belongs to our God who is seated on the throne, and to the Lamb!"

11 And all the angels stood around the throne and around the elders and the four living creatures, and they fell on their faces before the throne and worshiped God, singing,

12 "Amen! Blessing and glory and wisdom
and thanksgiving and honor
and power and might
be to our God forever and ever! Amen."

As the heavenly liturgy of 5:8-14 introduced the opening of the seals, this liturgy forms the climax to the unfolding events. The "great multitude" is not a group distinct from the 144,000 of 7:4-8; it is the same group, now viewed beyond the great tribulation: the Church triumphant in heaven. In keeping with John's consistent outlook, these, the victors, are presented as happy here and now. They stand before God and Lamb, celebrating a heavenly Feast of Tabernacles. The Feast of Tabernacles, marking the grape harvest, was the most joyous of Jewish feasts. The symbolism is clear; in our terms we might depict these martyrs as celebrating, in heaven, a perpetual Christmas. The vision is proleptic: it anticipates the future destiny of those now faithfully enduring tribulation. The angels, the countless host of 5:11, join in the heavenly liturgy, first by adding their "Amen" to the prayer of the faithful and then with their own doxology.

8:3-4

3 Another angel with a golden censer came and stood at the altar; he was given a great quantity of incense to offer with the prayers of all the saints on the golden altar that is before the throne.

4 And the smoke of the incense, with the prayers of the saints, rose before God from the hand of the angel.

"When the Lamb opened the seventh seal, there was silence in heaven for about half an hour" (8:1). The seventh seal would suggest the End. Instead, there is a liturgical silence: a ritual anticipation of the trumpet plagues (6:1-11:19) which are introduced by heavenly worship (8:3-4). Before the seven angels of the plagues (8:2) can sound their sinister trumpets, another angel appears on the scene, one who officiates as priest in the heavenly temple and offers incense there. The prayers of the saints are the prayers of the martyrs of 6:9-10. While Revelation never directly refers to the worship of the earthly Church, Christians would recognize their prayers in the incense rising before the heavenly throne.

11:15-19

15 Then the seventh angel blew his trumpet, and there were loud voices in heaven, saying,

"The kingdom has become the kingdom of our Lord
and of his Messiah,
and he will reign forever and ever."

16 Then the twenty-four elders who sit on their thrones before God fell on their faces and worshiped God,

17 singing,

"We give you thanks, Lord God Almighty,
who are and who were,
for you have taken your great power
and begun to reign.

18 The nations raged,
but your wrath has come,
and the time for judging the dead,
for rewarding your servants, the prophets
and saints and all who fear your name,
both small and great,
and for destroying those who destroy the earth."

19 Then God's temple in heaven was opened, and the ark of his covenant was seen within his temple; and there were flashes of lightning, rumblings, peals of thunder, an earthquake, and heavy hail.

The loud voices in heaven (11:15) contrast with the liturgical silence of 8:1. The heavenly liturgy (11:15-18) corresponds to that of 7:9-12. It closes the eschatological drama of the trumpets. The loud voices of praise in heaven are the voices not only of elders, living creatures and angelic choirs (4:8; 5:11-12) but also, surely, of the "great multitude" (7:9-10). The canticle of 11:17-18 is put in the mouth of the twenty-four elders. These thank and glorify God, who has at last manifested his almighty power: the kingdom of God has come. Until now God is he "who is, who was, and who is to come" (1:4,8; 4:8). But here there is no "who is to come" (see 16:5): he has come; his reign has begun.

The time has come for judging, for rewarding, and for destroying. The "destroyers of the earth" (the dragon and the beasts, chapters 12-13) are not to be confused with the "inhabitants of the earth," who are human dupes of the *destroyers*. The "wrath" of God is aimed primarily at the "destroyers"; it is only when they are at last removed that humankind can finally be at rest.

12:10-12

10 Then I heard a loud voice in heaven,
proclaiming:

"Now have come the salvation and the power
and the kingdom of our God
and the authority of his Messiah,
for the accuser of our comrades has been
thrown down,
who accuses them day and night before our
God.

11 But they have conquered him by the blood of
the Lamb
and by the word of their testimony,
for they did not cling to life even in the face of
death.

12 Rejoice then, you heavens
and those who dwell in them!
But woe to the earth and the sea,
for the devil has come down to you

with great wrath,
    because he knows that his time is short!"

The fall of the dragon is dramatized in 12:7-12; although Michael is represented as casting Satan out of heaven, it really is the victory of Christ—victory won *on the cross*. The hymn of verses 10-12 is a commentary on the narrative of verses 7-9 and 13-17. Everything that John sees in heaven is the counterpart of some earthly reality. When the victory is being won in heaven, Christ is on earth on the cross. Because he is part of the earthly reality, he cannot at the same time be part of the heavenly symbolism. Here, in fact, John has reversed the standard heaven-earth relationship. Normally, in apocalyptic, heaven is the "real" world, with earth a reflection of it. In our case, the victory is won, by Jesus, in *this* world, a victory that brings about the defeat of evil forces in the heavenly world. It should be noted that, here and throughout, "heaven" is not *the* heaven that is the abode of God; Jewish speculation posited many levels in heaven.

The heavenly hymn (vv 10-12) extols the saving power of God, manifest in the victory of Christ. Significantly, it is "our comrades" (or better, "our brothers and sisters"; the Greek *adelphoi*, "brothers," is obviously inclusive), object of his accusations, who have conquered Satan. Their victory, won "by the blood of the Lamb" is through the laying down of their lives. Despite the bellicose language and imagery of Revelation, John maintains that the war against evil was fought and won on the cross. The brothers and sisters have "conquered." Yes, indeed, but to conquer, in the case of Christ and Christians, is to die. "Conquer" never designates vindictive action against the enemies of Christ or of Christians. Jesus, silent before the Roman procurator, faithful unto death, won his victory. Jesus conquered through suffering and weakness rather than by might. There can be no other Christian victory, thus

95

the heavenly defeat of the dragon is signaled as the victory of the "brothers and sisters"—faithful Christians. The victims become victors. This is a factor that tempers the violent imagery of the work.

15:2-4

1 Then I saw another portent in heaven, great and amazing: seven angels with seven plagues, which are the last, for with them the wrath of God is ended.

2 And I saw what appeared to be a sea of glass mixed with fire, and those who had conquered the beast and its image and the number of its name, standing beside the sea of glass with harps of God in their hands.

3 And they sing the song of Moses, the servant of God, and the song of the Lamb:

"Great and amazing are your deeds,
Lord God the Almighty!
Just and true are your ways,
King of the nations!

4 Lord, who will not fear
and glorify your name?
For you alone are holy.
All nations will come
and worship before you,
for your judgments have been revealed."

The seven plagues (chapters 15-16) are the last because "with them the wrath of God is ended." The seer is once more in heaven and sees again the "sea of glass" of 4:6, but this time it is a sea "mixed with fire": symbol of God's judgment. Beside the heavenly sea stand the victors; they have been victorious in the same manner as the "Lamb standing as if it had been slaughtered" (5:6). Though termed "song of Moses," this song of the victors, unlike the song of Exodus 15:1-18, is not one of triumph over enemies; it is solely praise of God. Again, we are challenged to question John's alleged vindictiveness, all the more so because the second part of the song (v 4) holds out hope that the nations, in view of the righteous deeds of the Lord, will fear him—that is, acknowledge him—and render him homage and worship. In other words, God is king of the nations and the nations will come to acknowledge him as their king.

19:1-8

1 After this I heard what seemed to be the loud voice of a great multitude in heaven, saying:

"Hallelujah!
Salvation and glory and power to our God,

2   for his judgments are true and just;
he has judged the great whore
    who corrupted the earth with her
        fornication,
and he has avenged on her the blood of his
    servants."

3 Once more they said:

"Hallelujah!
The smoke goes up from her forever and ever!"

4 And the twenty-four elders and the four living creatures fell down and worshiped God who is seated on the throne, saying,

"Amen! Hallelujah!"

5 And from the throne came a voice saying,

"Praise our God,
    all you his servants,
and all who fear him,
    small and great."

6 Then I heard what seemed to be the voice of a
great multitude, like the sound of many waters
and like the sound of mighty thunderpeals,
crying out,

"Hallelujah!
For the Lord God
the Almighty reigns.

7 Let us rejoice and exult
and give him the glory,
for the marriage of the Lamb has come,
and his bride has made herself ready;

8 to her it has been granted to be clothed
with fine linen, bright and pure"—

for the fine linen is the righteous deeds of the
saints.

John stresses the occasion of this heavenly victory
song: execution of judgment on Babylon (Rome) for her
crimes of idolatry and blood-guilt. The great harlot, who
had seduced the whole earth and had become drunk
on the blood of martyrs (17:1-6), has met her just
desserts.

The elders and the living creatures (last mentioned
in 14:3) add their "Amen" to the canticle of the angels
(see 5:14). A voice from the throne summons all servants of God to praise the Lord; the vast throng of
victors takes up the hymn. They rejoice that their
often-repeated prayer—"Your kingdom come"—has
been answered: the Lord reigns! The victors are invited
guests at the marriage feast of the Lamb. His bride has
made herself ready—but her wedding gown is his gift.
And yet it is woven of the righteous deeds of God's
people. Thus, it appears that while the bride is the
Church, the wedding guests are the members of the
Church, and their deeds are her bridal dress. The
seeming jumble of John's imagery here holds a salutary

reminder. He reminds us that the Church has no existence apart from the living community (a living community, too, beyond death) of Christian men and women.

22:16-17

16 "It is I, Jesus, who sent my angel to you with this testimony for the churches. I am the root and the descendant of David, the bright morning star."

17 The Spirit and the bride say, "Come."
And let everyone who hears say, "Come."
And let everyone who is thirsty come.
Let anyone who wishes take the water of life
as a gift.

The whole of Revelation is "the revelation of Jesus Christ," his "testimony" made known, through an angel, to John (1:1). At the close, Jesus sets the seal of approval on the fidelity of his prophet. Jesus is both root and branch; he combines all the messianic claims of the Davidic family; he is the "beginning and end" (22:13) of the whole messianic economy.

Inspired by the Spirit, the Church (the "bride") prays its *marana tha*, "Our Lord, Come!" The Church (the earthly Church) responds with eager joy to the Lord's announcement of his coming (22:12). The prayer is to be caught up by every hearer of the book (see 1:3). Attention turns to the community: "everyone who is thirsty" is invited to come to Christ. In 3:20 we may observe a eucharistic flavor in the promise of a meal shared by Christ with Christians. It would seem that there is eucharistic interest here too in this offer of the water of life. The invitation of Spirit and Bride blends into an invitation to eucharistic fellowship.

Liturgical Dialogues

Revelation was explicitly designed to be read aloud in the liturgy (1:3), and it is spangled with heavenly liturgies. It has been plausibly suggested that 1:4-8 might be read as a liturgical dialogue (see U. Vanni, *Biblica* 57 (1976): 460f).

1:4-8   LECTOR: Grace to you and peace from him who is and who was and who is to come...and from Jesus Christ, the faithful witness, the firstborn of the dead, and the ruler of the kings of the earth.

ASSEMBLY: To him who loves us and freed us from our sins by his blood, and made us to be a kingdom, priests serving his God and Father, to him be glory and dominion forever and ever. Amen.

LECTOR:

Look! He is coming with the clouds;
    every eye will see him,
even those who pierced him;
    and on his account all the tribes of the
    earth will wail.

ASSEMBLY: So it is to be. Amen.

LECTOR: "I am the Alpha and the Omega," says the Lord God, who is and who was and who is to come, the Almighty.

22:17

Paralleling the liturgical reconstruction of 1:4-8, 22:17 could follow a similar pattern and become, plausibly, a liturgical invitation to Eucharist:

The Spirit and the bride say, "Come."

And let everyone who hears say, "Come."
And let everyone who is thirsty come.
Let anyone who wishes take take the water of
life as a gift.

Revelation in the Contemporary Church's Prayer

Revelation does *not* figure largely in the liturgical prayer of the contemporary Church. In the lectionary it provides the second reading for Sundays 2-7 of Easter in Year C. In the Divine Office it provides canticles for Evening Prayer.

		Lectionary	*Divine Office*
Sunday	2	1:9-13,17-19	4:11; 5:9,10,12
	3	5:11-14	11:17-18
	4	7:9,14-17	12:10b-12a
	5	21:1-5	15:3-4
	6	21:10-14,22-23	19:1-2,5-7
	7	22:12-14,16-17,20	

The canticles have been treated above. Here are brief commentaries on the Sunday readings.

Second Sunday of Easter (1:9-13,17-19)

A brief prologue (1:1-3) introduces Revelation as a letter of the prophet John, a letter meant to be read at a liturgical assembly. John is conscious of being spokesperson of the supreme pastor of the Church: Christ. John is "brother" of those to whom he writes. Like them he is incorporated into Jesus as he shares fully their destiny of suffering and glory. And he shares with them "patient endurance." This term occurs seven times in Revelation (1:9; 2:2,3,19; 3:10; 13:10; 14:12); it is the characteristic virtue of the persecuted. It is grounded on faith in Jesus, the Lord who comes; it is inspired by the certainty of his love; it is marked by strength of soul which enables one to endure, and it finds expression in the bearing of trials in steadfastness under tribulation.

It is a matter of first importance that John's opening statement about the "one in human form" (literally, "like a son of man"), his introduction of Christ, is that he saw him among the "lamps" (or "lampstands"), that is, among the churches (the seven churches, symbolized by lamps, to which the message of John is addressed). The risen and ascended Lord is no absentee landlord. He is present in his earthly communities; he knows their "works." It is in his name that John speaks his prophetic messages. The overall effect of the vision is one of terrifying majesty; John's reaction is that of Daniel (Dan 10:8-9). Yet, this majestic figure remains the Jesus of the gospel, and John hears again his comforting, "Do not be afraid" (see Mk 6:50; Mt 28:10).

This inaugural vision effectively brings out the oracular character of the first part of Revelation, for it is closely parallel to the inaugural visions of the Jewish Scripture prophets (see Isa 6; Jer 1; Ezek 1-3). But where the latter proceeded to speak in the name of Yahweh ("thus says Yahweh"), John will make known the "revelation of Jesus Christ." And, since in his eyes, the symbolic seven reaches beyond the communities he addresses immediately, his message—the message of the Lord—has meaning for the Church until the end of time.

Third Sunday of Easter (5:11-14)

Chapter five of Revelation depicts a transfer of power; God hands over to the Lamb (the crucified and risen Christ) a sealed scroll, since the Lamb alone has been found worthy to open that sealed book. The reading gives the close of the chapter, part of the first of the heavenly hymns so frequent in the book. The "one seated on the throne" is named frequently throughout: God as king and judge. The "living creatures" are, in Jewish tradition, the four angels who direct the physical world; therefore they symbolize the created universe. (The identification of the "living creatures" with the evangelists is wholly fanciful). The elders, twenty-four in number, are the heavenly representatives of the earthly Church. The living creatures and the elders had sung a hymn to the Lamb (5:9-10); now a new feature is introduced: the praise of a countless host of angels (see Dan 7:10). The first four words of the doxology concern the Lamb's dominion; the other three express the adoration of the angels (5:12). Finally the whole of creation joins in the great canticle of praise (5:13-14). John *hears* the voice of the great acclamation; to it the four living creatures give their "Amen"—and the elders worship.

Fourth Sunday of Easter (7:9,14-17)

This "great multitude" is not a group distinct from the 144,000 (itself a "great multitude") of 7:4-8; it is the same group viewed under a different aspect: it is the Church triumphant in heaven. More particularly, for John, these are the Christian martyrs. In keeping with his consistent outlook they are presented as happy here and now; they stand before God and the Lamb, celebrating a heavenly Feast of Tabernacles. (Tabernacles was the most joyous of Hebrew feasts).

As martyrs sharing in Christ's victorious death, they have immediately received their white robes of victory (6:11); palm branches are a symbol of triumph and joy. But the martyrs stand for all faithful Christians and in their priestly role (1:6) they serve God, adding their necessary human voice to the prayer of creation (4:8).

In their heavenly Feast of Tabernacles there is no need for the martyrs to construct their own booths (Lev 23:33-36); God himself will be their tabernacle, their tent (*skéne*)—there is a probable reference to the *shekinah*, the immediate presence of God in the Temple (see Rev 21:3). The texts of Isaiah (49:10; 52:8), which refer to the happy return from the Babylonian exile, find their fulfillment in the shepherding of the Lamb who leads his own sheep to the unfailing fountains of life (Rev 7:16-17). For, in startling and beautiful paradox, the Lamb has become a shepherd. In the Fourth Gospel the Lamb of God (Jn 1:29,36) is also the Good Shepherd (10:14-16).

Fifth Sunday of Easter (21:1-5)

The closing part of Revelation opens with the vision of a new heaven and a new earth, the setting of the new Jerusalem. The former creation has passed away (20:11) and all evil has been destroyed; now is the final phase of God's plan. The structure of Revelation 21:1-2 is modeled on Isaiah 65:17-19: the appearance of a new world, the disappearance of the former things, and the manifestation of a new Jerusalem. The new Jerusalem is a city of heavenly origin, a city "whose builder and maker is God" (Heb 11:10; 12:22; Gal 4:26). Jerusalem was an accepted figure of the people of Israel, the people of God; it was a tangible sign of the covenant, the focus of Jewish faith and hope. To present a new Jerusalem was, in the language of imagery, to proclaim the election of a new people and the sealing of a new covenant. The two-fold image of "city" and "bride" is traditional; in this chapter John combines the images, slipping abruptly from one to the other.

In the New Jerusalem sorrow and pain will have no place; the total defeat of the satanic forces, graphically described in 19:11-20:10, has brought to an end all that made up a world of sin. Now is fulfilled the promise of the most intimate sharing of life between God and his people—a constant theme in Jewish Scripture. Then, God speaks. He speaks the creative word which calls the new world into being; it is the process of re-creation by which the old is transformed into the new. God is at the beginning and at the end. He is at the origin of all and at the end of all. All things have tended toward God, and now all things are found in him.

Sixth Sunday of Easter (21:10-14,22-23)

Revelation closes with a majestic view of the New Jerusalem, the heavenly Church of the future, the true kingdom of God. John's model for his presentation of the New Jerusalem is Ezekiel's vision of the messianic kingdom (Ezek 40-48). That prophet was carried, in vision, from Babylon to Israel and was set upon a very high mountain; there he saw, opposite him, "a structure like a city": the temple of the future. Fittingly, the heavenly city of John has heavenly gatekeepers, and the gates of the New Jerusalem bear the names of the tribes of Israel (Rev 21:12). When he goes on to tell us that the names of the twelve apostles are inscribed on the wall's foundations (v 14), John asserts the continuity of the Christian Church with Israel. A city which is built on the foundation of the apostles is built on the apostolic tradition, the revelation of God of which the apostles were eyewitnesses and guarantors.

We might expect John's glowing description of the city (21:15-21) to be followed by a particularly striking description of its temple (the temple was the glory of the earthly Jerusalem) Instead—a brilliant touch—we learn that there is no temple, nor any need of one: God himself dwells there with the Lamb (vv 22-23). Now, indeed, "the dwelling of God is with mortals" (v 3) and the glory of his presence pervades the city (vv 11,18), making the New Jerusalem one vast temple. This is reminiscent of 7:15, where God himself is the tent at the heavenly Feast of Tabernacles, for the liturgy of that feast appears to be present to the seer throughout our passage. A nightly ceremony with bright lights and rejoicing was a feature of Tabernacles. In the new city the Lamb will give light by night and God will replace the sun. God is not hidden as he was in the temple of old.

Seventh Sunday of Easter (22:12-14,16-17,20)

Like the Fourth Gospel and the first epistle of John, Revelation also closes with an appendix or epilogue, giving the last words of the angel, the seer and the Lord (22:6-21). The lectionary reading is content with the words of the Lord. The time has come for "rewarding God's servants." Christ comes exercising a divine prerogative; he comes "bringing his reward with him." It is perfectly natural that the earthly paradise of Genesis 2 should become a symbol of heavenly blessedness. The tree of life is within the city, so one must pass through the gates to reach it; the beatitude (v 14) makes eternal life accessible to all but only through the blood of the Lamb, the cross of Christ.

The whole of Revelation is "the revelation of Jesus Christ," his "testimony," made known through an angel to John (1:1); it is a message for the whole Church (1:4). At the close (22:16) Jesus sets the seal of approval on the fidelity of his prophet. The final verses (22:17-21) have an unmistakable liturgical ring. The Spirit inspires the Church (the earthly Church) to respond with eager joy to the Lord's announcement of his coming. While the hearer welcomes the coming of Christ, "the one who is thirsty" is invited to come to Christ. And Christ, who bears his own solemn testimony to the contents of the book, assures his Church that he is coming soon (v 20). It is a response to the earnest prayer of the Church (v 17) and a link with the promise at the beginning of the book: "Look, he is coming with the clouds" (1:7). But this time the promise stands in the liturgical setting of the Eucharist. "Come Lord Jesus" is a rendering of the Aramaic *marana tha* ("Our Lord, Come!" [1 Cor 16:22]) of the liturgy. There is an intimate link between the Eucharist and the coming of Christ: "For as often as you eat this bread and drink the cup you proclaim the Lord's death until he comes" (1 Cor 11:26).

For Personal and Group Reflection

1. Revelation was written for public reading in the liturgy. How does the Christian people's interpretation of scripture in liturgy differ from that of biblical scholars?

2. Revelation stresses the centrality of worship for Christian life just as Vatican Council II called us to liturgical renewal. Give examples of the ways in which liturgy has taken on a more important role in your own life.

3. Belonging to a "royal house of priests" (Rev 1:6), how do you individually and as a parish community exercise the priestly ministry of all the baptized?

4. John focuses on the celebration of a heavenly liturgy. Of those liturgies you have recently celebrated, which sticks in your mind as the most satisfying? Why was it so good? Which aspects of your parish liturgy do you find unsatisfying and why?

5. Silence is not only a key feature of liturgy but of all prayerfulness. Does silence have a place in your daily life?

6. For which triumphs should we praise God in our contemporary lives?

7. In places John seems vindictive and in other places rejoices in the hurt done to others. Is this Christian? If not, how do you explain it as being here in a book of the bible?

8. John speaks about heavenly liturgies and a new creation for which we are in preparation. How has reading Revelation challenged you to appreciate the communion of saints?

Chapter Six

Relevance for Contemporary Disciples

I f Revelation is seen only as crisis literature, written in the stress of active persecution, it is not easy to see that it can have much to say to our western churches. We do not live in an atmosphere of apocalyptic crisis. We certainly do not experience, or envisage, violent persecution. But, if we regard Revelation as a reflection of John's assessment of his world, we may see how and where it does address us. John was not coping with a situation of actual persecution. If there were to be "tribulation" on a grand scale, it would be in response to a radical Christian rejection of the status quo. Revelation does have something to say to our world—if we interpret its symbols in relation to our situation.

God Rules in Our Chaotic World

The Lamb

The great throne (4:2) dominates Revelation, a constant reminder that God rules even in our chaotic world. The Almighty God has a purpose and plan for this world. In dealing with the human world God will not proceed without cooperation of humankind. God sought an agent—and found him in the Lamb (chapter 5). This Messiah, scion of David, is the Lamb *who was slain*. Our Almighty God manifests his power on the cross. In the cross, in the blood of the Lamb, he holds out salvation to all. The Lamb, as the manifestation, as the very presence, of our gracious God, is worthy of our honor and worship. He is worthy precisely as the slain Lamb, as the crucified One. Like Paul and Mark, John too, in his manner, proposes a *theologia crucis*, a theology of the cross. That comforting—if challenging—theme threads through his work.

John's opening address in 1:4-8 is full of comfort. We are assured that our God is the everlasting, the Almighty. But we Christians meet this awesome God in the one who laid down his life for us. John puts, in his manner, what Paul had already declared: "God proves his love for us in that while we were still sinners Christ died for us" (Rom 5:8). Once slaves of sin, we have been set free: "if the Son makes you free, you will be free indeed" (Jn 8:36). Christian privilege brings its challenging obligation: priestly concern for the whole of humankind (Rev 1:6). But nothing less should inspire those who serve the God who is God of all.

John's vision (1:9-20) of the risen Lord is dramatic counterpart of the closing declaration of Matthew's Lord: "Remember, I am with you always, to the end of the age" (Mt 28:20). We also have the comfort of his presence in our midst—comfort, but challenge too, as the messages to the churches underline. We acknowledge this challenge as we worship him as our Lord. But never should we fear in his presence (1:17). He is the one who lifts from us even the deep-rooted fear of death for he, the Living One, is Victor over Death (1:18).

The Challenge of the Way

The challenge of the Way remains. There is an incompatibility between wholehearted following of Christ and the standards of a world unenlightened by the gospel. There is the danger that Christians can settle, too readily, for a "reasonable" accommodation. It is the charism of a prophet to see to the heart of things. Only the starkest words can match his uncomplicated vision. The genuine prophet will speak a message of comfort, based on the faithfulness of God, but it will never be a comfortable message. John's prophetic messages to the churches (chapters 2-3) urge us to look to ourselves, to our contemporary Ephesus and Philadelphia and Laodicea. The beast in our world—in our western world at least—is not as openly oppressive as the beast of John's world. It may be all the more dangerous because more insidious.

Perhaps the relentless John is right after all: there is no compromise. And from these messages, too, we can draw a comfort that comes from a better grasp of the overall Christian Scripture situation. We learn that our first brothers and sisters in the faith are no different from ourselves. They, as we, in human frailty, had to live out their faith in an unsympathetic, often hostile, world. They, as we, had their doubts and their fears. They, as we, had to hear the warning: "in the world you have tribulation," and, despite every appearance to the contrary, had to cling, in hope, to the assurance: "Take courage; I have conquered the world!" (Jn 16:33).

111

The Destroyers

Over against God and Lamb stand the dragon and the beast. The dragon is the oppressive weight of sin bearing on humankind. It is many-faceted, but it is starkly manifest in greed in all its shapes, in particular, lust for power and control. The beast may be rampant capitalism, so cruelly impersonal, and our consumer culture, so shamelessly selfish. The slogan of unbridled affluence is: Who is like the beast? (13:4).

Authority of the Lamb

A great contrast in Revelation is between the throne of God and the throne of the beast—ultimately the throne of the dragon (13:14). The question is all about authority, more especially, the exercise of authority. God is *Pantocrator*, the Almighty, but divine authority is visible in the Lamb. And Jesus had stated his position without ambiguity and with studied emphasis: "You know that among the Gentiles those whom they recognize as their rulers lord it over them, and their great ones are tyrants over them. But it is not so among you....For the Son of Man came not to be served but to serve, and to give his life a ransom for many" (Mk 10:42-45). The victory of God, the ultimate authority, is the cross of the Lamb. In light of that, John viewed any authority based on power as demonic. We really must ask ourselves if the Christian churches have done as Jesus demanded or have followed the pattern of the Gentiles. We must discern and challenge the demonic in our ecclesiastical structures. This is where a hearkening to John's message will be costly. We need not doubt that challenge will bring *thlipsis*, "tribulation." Faithfulness to this "revelation of Jesus Christ" demands that we take a stand against power structures which distort the stark message of the Lamb, the sword of his mouth, the word of the cross.

"War broke out in heaven" (Rev 12:7)—does this, somehow, underwrite our human propensity for strife and war? It has been too easy for us to conjure up the concept of "just" war; we have not shrunk from the notion of "holy" war. John had already painted, in somber colors, the hideous reality of war (6:1-8). And, throughout his book, Christians are never the perpetrators but always the victims of violence. After all, it is the Lamb who, by breaking the first seal, unleashes the plagues, the Lamb who was "slain from the foundation of the world" (13:8). There is no human violence against evil. There is resistance—something quite different—*costly* resistance: "for they did not cling to life even in the face of death" (12:11).

Conquest of the Beast

"In amazement the whole earth followed the beast" (13:3). A great power, notably a totalitarian power, may appear to have an impressive permanence and a seeming invincibility. Yet, historically, empires have collapsed with dramatic suddenness. In our day we have witnessed the eclipse of a "superpower." But, then, one empire succeeds another. The "beast" may assume many guises. Assault on God's people—the nature of the beast—may be brutal; it may, too, be an insidious infiltration, a weakening of the nerve of the Church. If John calls for endurance and faith in face of active persecution, he calls for no less endurance in face of what he regards as the threat of an alien culture; witness his messages to the churches. This may well be a challenge to us in our contemporary world.

For John the beast is Rome. The second puppet beast (13:11-17) represented false religion—specifically, the emperor-cult. Historically, even religion that is "authentic" has too often worn aspects of the beast. The word of Jesus stands as perennial challenge: "The sabbath was made for humankind, and not humankind for the sabbath" (Mk 2:27). Religion is for men and women, not men and women for religion. The beast "caused" people to act; it forced people to conform (13:14-16). Can we honestly deny that religion, even our Christian religion, has been tyrannical? Can we deny that it does not still, in some measure, dominate? We have it on the authority of Jesus not only to reject but actively to oppose this abuse of religion. To take such a stand may cost us dearly. Jesus paid the price.

Our western civilization has much that is admirable, but is it really as robust as it seems? It is founded on capitalism, an economic system that may be defensible—within limits. In practice, the greed of our consumer-oriented society oversteps the borders of justice. Ask the third world! The great business corporations are motivated almost solely by profit; they oppress, directly and indirectly. Pollution of the environment, result of an unbridled exploitation of natural resources, itself spurred by pursuit of gain, is a cancer at the vitals of our planet. Nations, even the more wealthy and powerful nations, do not have the political will to confront a dire situation with courage. Greed is a particularly nasty form of evil. John's striking image of beast and kings consuming the Great City (17:16) holds a message for us. He depicts the civilization of his day as being fatally threatened from within itself. It is not difficult to diagnose a malaise at the heart of our world. Is it too late to save the patient?

Faithful Witness

John, in light of the great tribulation which he expects imminently to break, has to put before the Christians of his concern a prospect of violent death. Their *hypomoné*, "patient endurance," may—most likely will—demand faithfulness unto death. He takes care, then, to stress the blessedness of such fidelity.

The faithful will pass, immediately beyond death, into their heavenly rest. This is all very well, but the oppressor cannot be permitted to escape unscathed. The blood of the victims must be avenged; justice must prevail. "How long...before you judge?" (6:10). This is human sentiment, but it does underline the truth that, in God's world, evil must not, cannot, prevail. This "how long" betrays understandable human impatience at a situation in which evil does seem to win the day. Our longing and our prayer will not spur God to violent action against evil. God has already taken the action that underwrites the total root of evil. His deed is the cross. We are back to the Lamb.

The Victors

One should keep in mind that, for John, the victors are those who "did not cling to life even in the face of death" (12:11). The "sealing," assurance of divine concern (7:2-4), will entail no "rapture" of the elect. They will be "caught up" indeed, but caught up in the tribulation, helpless victims—helpless as their Lord on his cross. For them, as for him, there will be no legion of angels (see Mt 26:53). We must look for no miracle, apart from the abiding miracle of our God's loving care.

"Was it not necessary that the Christ should suffer these things and then enter into his glory?" (Lk 24:26) the risen Lord rebuked the uncomprehending Emmaus disciples. In Revelation John pictures the glory of the victors beyond the tribulation (7:9-17). They have triumphed, but not on their own. Victory is theirs because, and only because, the Lamb had first conquered. It is a conviction shared by the fourth evangelist—"apart from me you can do nothing" (Jn 15:5)—and by Paul—"I can do all things through him who strengthens me" (Phil 4:13). It is a lesson we need to take to heart. A glorious destiny awaits us, yes, but precisely as followers of the Lamb. While we do not share John's expectation of imminent eschatological tribulation, we may well be failing to discern a more insidious and pervasive challenge. John saw through the Empire of his day, discerned its distorted standard of values. We have become so much part of our contemporary empire, the lifestyle of the western world, that we may no longer be stirred, excited, by prospect of heavenly joy.

Witness

"Jesus Christ, the faithful witness" (1:5) bore courageous witness before Jewish religious authority and the Roman procurator—and paid the price. The "two witnesses" (11:3-13) stand for his faithful ones who are prepared to walk his way and, like him, pay the price. They earn the hatred of "the beast that comes up from the bottomless pit" (11:7). We, as Christians, are urged to be witnesses in our turn. In our western world at least—it is not so elsewhere—we have little fear that we will be summarily slaughtered and our bodies left to lie where we fall. By and large, our witness is so discreet that "the inhabitants of the earth" are not troubled. We, for the most part, blend decently into the background of our culture; we are wholly respectable. John would not rate our Christian witness very highly. Nor, one fears, does he who walks among the lamps!

To be a witness to Christ is a life-time task. To be a prophet, Christ's spokesperson, is a challenging task. There is, indeed, the privilege of service, but the cost is high. Every person who strives to preach and teach the word of God knows at once fulfillment and frustration. There is no more worthwhile service. But one must discern the pain that ripples through the pages of Christian Scripture, the pain of the preachers of the good news; that word is not heeded.

God offers salvation, but on what terms? On no terms but God's. This is not being dictatorial; on the contrary,

God's offer of salvation is based on a radical refusal to dominate. The kingdom of God is the free kingdom of wholly liberated women and men. Revelation, like every Scripture text, is text for humankind. "Plagues" are God's reaction to evil and sin, reaction envisaged and depicted in human mode. God's will is always salvation.

God's Reaction to Evil and Sin

Plagues

Revelation can easily give an impression of implacable divine wrath—even a strong flavor of vindictiveness. A first step toward a proper grasp of this aspect of the book might be a consideration of the Genesis flood story. There too, at first sight, Yahweh/God is stirred to violent action against sin and sinners. The flood story is myth, a story of fundamental symbols which are vehicles of ultimate meaning. Myth speaks timeless truth, truth vital for human existence; it brings out the *super*natural dimension of events. In the flood story we see the holy God's radical incompatibility with evil— God's grief over human sin. The flood is not an historical event; it is a mythical event. Myth expresses truth. The flood story assures us that God will have the last word: "never again shall there be a flood to destroy the earth" (Gen 9:13). Revelation, too, is myth. The plagues exist in vision only. The great battle of Armageddon (Rev 19:11-21; see 16:16) is not an historical but a mythical battle. None of the violence of the plagues is literal violence against our world; it is violence in visionary scenes of the future, couched in metaphorical language. Again, just as there is no "real" flood, there were no "real" plagues of Egypt, and there were not, nor will be, "real" plagues of Revelation. John is convinced of universal human sinfulness (Christians also are sinners [1:5]). The eschatological terrors are an expression of his sense of justice. That is why God and Lamb are the source of violence; Christians can only be victims, not perpetrators of violence (13:9-10). After all, it is the Lamb, by breaking the first seal, who unleashes the plagues—for all three cycles are interconnected— the Lamb "who was slain from the foundation of the world." There is *no* human violence against evil.

Evil

There is, in our world, an oppressive burden of evil. Awful things happen every day. It is tempting to look to forces beyond humankind; indeed, such has been the human propensity. Perhaps just here is the truly "demonic" dimension of evil. To look to an influence beyond ourselves, and an influence, for that matter, more malignant and more powerful than we, is to evade our responsibility. It is more honest, and potentially more healing, to acknowledge our responsibility. True, there is an influence that weighs upon us, but it is the inherited burden of human perversity. "The inclination of the human heart is evil from youth" (Gen 8:21): evil is within humanness, not outside of it. For evil is not only the absence of good; it is, more precisely, the absence of everything authentically human. Satan is a powerful symbol (see Rev 12:3-4,13-18), representing the whole gamut of evil and its infectious presence in the human race. The Christian hope is the restoration of all things in Christ—meaning the absolute end of evil itself. The "lake of fire" consumes even "the dragon" (20:10,14).

The motivation of the plagues is not vindictiveness; they are a summons to *metanoia*. But, as with Pharaoh (Ex 7:13,22), this purpose was not achieved: humankind did not repent. See Wisdom 12:20—"You punished with such great care and indulgence the enemies of your servants and those deserving of death, granting

them time and opportunity to give up their wickedness"—and Romans 2:4-5—"Do you despise the riches
of his kindness and forbearance and patience? Do you
not realize that God's kindness is meant to lead you to
repentance?"

It is the biblical view that idolatry is the root of all
evil (see Rev 9:20-21). The first temptation is to be like
God (see Gen 3:50); the first sin is to attempt to act
accordingly. The human being is creature and can
never be other. Our destiny—the glorious status of
children of God—is achieved only with God, never in
defiance of God. The generous Father, who yearns for
our salvation, summons us to *metanoia*. This means,
above all, turning from our "idolatry," from our vain
endeavors to go it alone. We become what our God
wants us to be in his way and together with him, not
otherwise (see 15:3-4).

Mercy

Surely John has invited us to view the seven plagues
of Trumpets about to be unleashed (15:5-8) against his
background portrait of a God who thinks only in terms
of salvation (15:3-4). For a Christian, can there be any
other God than he? Otherwise, what could one make
of a God who did not spare his own Son? What does
one make of the folly of the cross? John is faced with
the enigma of an infinitely gracious God face to face
with human perversity. His problem—which is our
problem—is to face that riddle within our grossly limited human perspective. From a merely human point
of view the situation might seem uncomplicated. There
is right and there is wrong, and wrong calls for punishment. That human view is too simplistic. In his time,
David had made the wise decision: "Let us fall into the
hand of the Lord, for his mercy is great; but let me not
fall into human hands" (2 Sam 24:14). John's problem
was how to make his Christians measure up to the

tribulation which he foresaw. He felt that he had to jolt them into awareness of crisis—hence the bite of his imagery and language. We might ask ourselves how well we Christians perform in a largely post-Christian world. John perceived that the current ethos of his day was out of step with the message of Jesus. He was prepared to put his view, without remainder and without apology. Have we the courage to do as much?

The seven plagues of bowls (chapters 15-16) are "the last." As the plagues of Egypt were to bring Pharaoh to relent (see Ex 7:16-17; 8:1-4), to "let my people go," these plagues of bowls are a last effort to bring people to repent. Alas, evil is pervasive and deeply ingrained. But is evil ultimately resistant to the persistent love of God? It would seem that, as one looks more intently, John did not believe so. If he has to show, in a wholly unambiguous manner, that God does not countenance wickedness and oppression—"it grieves him to his heart" (Gen 6:6)—he will not hide the depth and range of God's forgiving and saving will.

Vigilance

The word of Jesus in Revelation 16:15—"See, I am coming like a thief! Blessed is the one who stays awake and is clothed, not going about naked and exposed to shame"—underlines the pastoral intent of the plague sequences. John's readers are left in no doubt that their God is wholly alive to the evil world in which they live. He seeks to warn them that evil may be, to some extent, veiled and seductive. They need to be alert, ever alert. Because we are not victims of persecution or discrimination on religious grounds, we are more vulnerable than were John's people to threats to our Christian standards. Their experience of intolerance, if not incipient persecution, conditioned them to measure their world by a "hermeneutic of suspicion." Our danger is that we become too receptive, gullible even.

We may readily accept current values as normative, not recognizing that they will not stand the scrutiny of the gospel. It would be well to ponder on the warning to Laodicea (3:15-19).

End of Evil

The dragon and the beasts are the forces ranged against God's people, the cynical exploiters of the rest of humankind—the "destroyers of the earth" (11:18). They are personifications of evil—in fact, the sum total of evil. In the "new heaven and new earth" (21:1) evil has no place. The "lake of fire" signifies its annihilation. A lurking evil, even though powerless to hurt, would take from the absolute triumph of Good. The disappearance is inevitable when it is understood that evil is nothing other than the absence of good.

All the violent action in Revelation wrought on the side of good is wrought by God and the Lamb. Indeed, it is all traced back to the Lamb. The breaking of the first seal (6:1) launched not only the first series of plagues but the other two as well—they are interconnected. As rider on the white horse, the Lamb launches the final, decisive battle. In all of this Christians endure—they do not take violent action against the worshipers of the beast. The message of Revelation is, in its apocalyptic dress, the message of Jesus. There must be a response to injustice, to oppression. That courageous response, which may and can demand the ultimate sacrifice, is always non-violent. That word speaks, paradoxically, through the violent imagery of Revelation. The only weapon of the oppressed is *hypomoné*, patient endurance. It is the weapon that, in the end, disarms evil. It seems that we have hardly begun to learn this lesson of Jesus. For that matter, have we Christians *really* learned any lesson of Jesus? Our record is not spectacular.

Greed

The dirges of kings and merchants and seafarers over stricken Rome are instructive (18:9-19). Self-interest is the name of the game. With the fall of Rome, the economic bottom had fallen out of their world. Up to now, they had been captains of commerce, manipulating and controlling world trade, and battening on it. We, in our western world, are proud of our standards and our lifestyle. The Empire was the source of Rome's wealth. The Sibylline Oracles document widespread unrest at taxation and exploitation. In our day there is concern that the first world owns or controls the great bulk of our earth's resources. A minority of the earth's inhabitants enjoy a lifestyle denied the rest.

In face, not only of affluence but, to an unacceptable degree, of excessive wealth, there is so much, far too much, grinding poverty. Justice demands that we of the first world be prepared to share. But that is not enough. We should come to realize just how far our prosperity is achieved and maintained at the cost of the poverty of others. We are being challenged to turn from self-interest.

As Christians we are being challenged by the gospel of Jesus Christ. Jesus taught and lived that the reality of God is revealed in the realization of more humanity between fellow human beings—giving drink to the thirsty, feeding the hungry, welcoming the stranger. Matthew's story of judgment (25:31-46) is focused on purely human concerns. The emphasis is on the needy person, the one in distress. What is at stake is an attitude toward the little ones, the humble and the needy. The criterion is not the standard of religion or cult; it is, starkly: Have I helped those in need?

As Christians, we might heed, and hearken to, the invitation: "Come out of her, my people" (Rev 18:4). We might begin by looking critically at the values of *our* world; we might measure it by the standard of the gospel. This is a painful task and, if we try to follow up on our findings, a costly task. Princes of commerce, mighty corporations, will not take kindly to challenge, will not welcome lower profit-margins. John tells us that greed, exploitation, and oppression are a cancer that will undermine and destroy every empire.

Salvation

"Books were opened...the book of life" (20:11-15). Our God has created us as free beings. He respects our freedom totally; that is why his grace is, so often, thoroughly disguised. We come, later, to discern his graciousness in our most painful episodes. Freedom is costly; it exacts the price of responsibility. We are responsible for our deeds—and for our omissions. Yet, all the while, our salvation is wholly grace: "Whoever does not receive the kingdom of God as a child will never enter it" (Mk 10:15). "Justified by his grace as a gift, through the redemption that is in Christ Jesus" (Rom 3:24). Responsible for what we do—we are judged by works; God is author of our salvation—we are saved by grace.

A common biblical image of future blessedness is the messianic feast. For John, in Christian terms, it is more specifically the marriage feast of the Lamb (Rev 19:6-9). He has occasion firmly to remind his Christians not only that they are invited guests at the marriage feast but that they are, at once, the bride herself and her bridal dress (19:7-8). The seeming jumble of John's imagery here holds a salutary reminder. "The Church" is bandied about so readily—and means many different things. Commonly, one thinks of the Church as an abstraction. Indeed, John might be said to share this view; he has the Woman sitting secure in the wilderness (12:6,14), while "her children" are being ravaged by the dragon (12:17). We should always respect the subtlety of his imagery. Here, at least, he makes clear that he is not dealing in abstractions. He reminds us that it is we, all of us together, who form the bride of Christ; it is our righteous deeds that clothe her. The Church is not some entity "out there" or "up there." It is not represented by a hierarchy; leaders in the Church have a servant role, not a representative role (see Mk 9:35; 10:42-45). It is, simply, the people of God: "all who fear him, small and great."

The New Jerusalem

The motif of the nearness of the End threads through the Book of Revelation. When he declares, at the beginning (1:3), that the time is near, John means that, in his view, the End is soon. Was he, then, mistaken? In one sense, obviously, yes. The End did not come in his day, nor has it occurred nineteen centuries later. What we might learn from him is a sense of urgency such as one finds also in Mark 9:1 and 13:30. For each of us *our* time is the only time we have to fulfill our calling, and our death is the end for us on earth. Our span of years is important for us and precious in the eyes of the Lord.

Eternal Life

What is eternal life with God? We, in our earthly existence, creatures of time and space, must perforce picture heavenly reality in terms of time and space. In 21:1-8 John has two central images. There will be a new heaven and a new earth (21:1). The dragon once had his place in the old heaven; he had ravaged the old earth (12:7-8,12). A creation that is, at last, utterly free of evil can only be *new*. Humankind is the summit of God's creation, his pride and joy (Gen 1:26-31). His destined home for humankind was the garden of delights (Gen 2:15). There will be a new home for humankind in the new creation: a *city*, city of God, the new Jerusalem (21:2-4,10-26). It is a heavenly city, yet a habitat of men and women. Heaven, however one may image it, must be a home for humankind—transformed humanity, indeed, but a world of truly whole women and men. It is a city without a temple. God and Lamb are there indeed, but not in the formality of a cultic setting. They dwell in the midst of their people.

Most dramatic of all is John's picture of the nations streaming into the New Jerusalem:

> The nations will walk by its light, and the kings
> of the earth will bring their glory into it. Its gates
> will never be shut by day—and there will be no
> night there. People will bring into it the glory
> and the honor of the nations (21:24-26).

They bring into it glory and honor—all that is worthy and lovely in human achievement. Though city of God, it is their city, true home of humankind. But these are the very kings and nations destroyed in the great battle! (19:11-21) God's saving purpose prevails.

Marana tha

John's glowing description is not only encouragement: it is challenge. We are summoned, here and now, to "lay aside every weight and the sin that clings so closely" (Heb 12:1; Rev 21:27). We are to look beyond evil to what is good in our world. We are to turn with confidence to the God who, though the One majestically seated on the throne, is the gracious God who wipes away every tear (7:17).

"See, I am coming soon" (22:7). It is an assurance that John's readers longed to hear. Life was not easy for them in the present. John's prospect of imminent tribulation augured much tougher times ahead. His promise to victors was all very well; the reality was that "conquering" meant dying! It was comforting to look to the One who was coming soon, "bringing his reward with him" (22:12). He was the one who had conquered by laying down his life. They, if they were faithful, would share his victory and his triumph. They look to his coming.

In the meantime, as they celebrate their Eucharist, they have his presence with them. They have the reminder of his victory and the assurance of his promise: "As often as you eat this bread and drink the cup, you proclaim the Lord's death until he comes" (1 Cor 11:26). They do not have to wait, bereft, for his final coming. Yet they long. "My desire is to depart and be with Christ, for that is far better" (Phil 1:23). It is in their going to him that the Lord will come to them—and to us! *Marana tha.*

Perhaps it is in our eucharistic celebration that Revelation might challenge us. It is on the night on which he was *delivered* up that the Lord took, gave thanks, and broke bread: "This is my body that is for you" (1 Cor 11:23-24). He is the Lamb who was slain. His death is victory for all. The Victim is the Victor. That is the "remembrance" of the Eucharist. That is the message of Revelation. Behind the surreal visions of the plagues is the Lamb. And with the Lamb is the One on the throne—the Father of our Lord Jesus Christ. "The *grace* of the Lord Jesus be with all" (Rev 22:21). This "revelation of Jesus Christ" is word of grace. Blessed is the one who hears...for "these words are trustworthy and true" (22:6).

For Personal and Group Reflection

1. More than anything else, John calls for a radical Christian rejection of the status quo. What in our status quo should be radically rejected?

2. Revelation frequently speaks about God's purpose and plan for the world.

What do you think is God's purpose
and plan for you?

3. John declares that we should never be
   afraid in the presence of God (Rev 1:17).
   Are you afraid of God. In what ways? Is
   this healthy or unhealthy? Is fear of
   God an authentic or unauthentic aspect
   of faith?

4. Christianity is a message of comfort
   that is never a comfortable message.
   What do you find comforting and what
   makes you uncomfortable about the
   Lord's call in this past year?

5. In Revelation, an authority of service is
   divine; an authority of power is
   demonic. What does this say to us
   about conversion in the forms of
   ecclesiastic structures and in the
   authority we exercise in our daily
   professional lives?

6. The beast's assault on God's people can
   be brutal or it can be an insidious
   infiltration. Which is it today, and
   where do you see it taking place?

7. John portrays the civilization of his day
   as corrupt within. Which are the
   corrupting influences of our own
   civilization?

8. John rejects the empire and sees
   satisfaction only in the new creation of
   God. Where do you find joy,
   satisfaction, and enthusiasm—in this
   world or in longing for the next?

9. Is the evil of our world from Satan or from ourselves? What are the implications of either answer?

10. In John's Revelation, the only weapon of the oppressed is patient endurance. Where do you feel called to patient endurance as an individual and as a member of the parish community?

Proposal for a Liturgical Presentation of Revelation

Revelation was originally meant to be read aloud at a liturgical celebration (Rev 1:3). If we are fully to appreciate the work, it could be that this is how we ought to hear it. It might, however, be too daunting to stage a dramatic presentation of the whole of Revelation. Here is an abridged version, with suggestions—no more than that—as to how it might be presented.

Opening Hymn (11:15,17)

The kingdom of the world has become the
   kingdom of our Lord
  and of his Messiah,
and he will reign forever and ever.

We give you thanks, Lord God Almighty,
  who are and who were,
for you have taken your great power
  and begun to reign.

Introduction (1:1-3)

Presider:

The revelation of Jesus Christ, which God gave him to show his servants what must soon take place; he made it known by sending his angel to his servant John, who testified to the word of God and to the testimony of Jesus Christ, even to all that he saw.

Blessed is the one who reads aloud the words of the prophecy, and blessed are those who hear and who keep what is written in it; for the time is near.

Prologue (1:4-8)

Presider:

Grace to you and peace from him who is and who was and who is to come, and from the seven spirits who are before his throne, and from Jesus Christ, the faithful witness, the firstborn of the dead, and the ruler of the kings of the earth.

Assembly:

To him who loves us and freed us from our sins by his blood, and made us to be a kingdom, priests serving his God and Father, to him be glory and dominion forever and ever. Amen.

Presider:

Look! He is coming with the clouds;
    every eye will see him,

even those who pierced him;
and on his account all the tribes of the
earth will wail.

Assembly:

So it is to be. Amen.

Presider:

"I am the Alpha and the Omega," says the Lord
God, who is and who was and who is to come,
the Almighty.

Vision (1:9-20)

Reader 1:

I, John, your brother who share with you in
Jesus the persecution and the kingdom and the
patient endurance, was on the island called
Patmos because of the word of God and the
testimony of Jesus. I was in the spirit on the
Lord's day, and I heard behind me a loud voice
like a trumpet saying, "Write in a book what you
see and send it to the seven churches, to
Ephesus, to Smyrna, to Pergamum, to Thyatira,
to Sardis, to Philadelphia, and to Laodicea."
Then I turned to see whose voice it was that
spoke to me, and on turning I saw seven golden
lampstands, and in the midst of the lampstands
I saw one like the Son of Man, clothed with a
long robe and with a golden sash across his
chest. His head and his hair were white as white
wool, white as snow; his eyes were like a flame
of fire, his feet were like burnished bronze,
refined as in a furnace, and his voice was like
the sound of many waters. In his right hand he
held seven stars, and from his mouth came a

sharp two-edged sword, and his face was like the sun shining with full force.

When I saw him, I fell at his feet as though dead. But he placed his right hand on me, saying, "Do not be afraid; I am the first and the last, and the living one. I was dead, and see, I am alive forever and ever; and I have the keys of Death and of Hades. Now write what you have seen, what is, and what is to take place after this. As for the mystery of the seven stars that you saw in my right hand, and the seven gold lampstands: the seven stars are the angels of the seven churches, and the seven lampstands are the seven churches."

Hymn (4:11)

You are worthy, our Lord and God,
   to receive glory and honor and power,
for you created all things,
   and by your will they existed and were
   created.

The Messages to the Churches

Ephesus (2:1-7)

Reader 2:

"To the angel of the church in Ephesus write: These are the words of him who holds the seven stars in his right hand, who walks among the seven gold lampstands:

"I know your works, your toil and patient endurance. I know that you cannot tolerate evil-doers; you have tested those who claim to

be apostles but are not, and have found them to
be false. I also know that you are enduring
patiently and bearing up for the sake of my
name, and that you have not grown weary. But I
have this against you: that you have abandoned
the love you had at first. Remember then from
what you have fallen; repent, and do the works
you did at first. If not, I will come to you and
remove your lampstand from its place, unless
you repent. Yet this to your credit: you hate the
works of the Nicolaitans, which I also hate. Let
anyone who has an ear listen to what the Spirit
is saying to the churches! To everyone who
conquers, I will give permission to eat from the
tree of life that is in the paradise of God."

Philadelphia (3:7-13)

Reader 3:

"And to the angel of the church in Philadelphia
write:

> These are the words of the holy one,
>> the true one,
> who has the key of David,
> who opens and no one will shut,
>> who shuts and no one opens:

"I know your works. Look, I have set before you
an open door, which no one is able to shut. I
know that you have but little power, and yet you
have kept my word and have not denied my
name. I will make those of the synagogue of
Satan who say that they are Jews and are not,
but are lying—I will make them come and bow
down before your feet, and they will learn that I
have loved you. Because you have kept my word
of patient endurance, I will keep you from the
hour of trial which is coming on the whole world

to test those inhabitants of the earth. I am coming soon; hold fast to what you have, so that no one may seize your crown. If you conquer, I will make you a pillar in the temple of my God; you will never go out of it. I will write on you the name of my God, and the name of the city of my God, the new Jerusalem that comes down from my God out of heaven, and my own new name. Let anyone with an ear listen to what the Spirit is saying to the churches."

Laodicea (3:14-22)

Reader 4:

"To the angel of the church in Laodicea write: The words of the Amen, the faithful and true witness, the origin of God's creation:

"I know your works; you are neither cold nor hot. I wish you were either cold or hot. So, because you are lukewarm, and neither cold not hot, I am about to spit you out of my mouth. For you say, 'I am rich, I have prospered, and I need nothing.' You do not realize that you are wretched, pitiable, poor, blind, and naked. Therefore I counsel you to buy from me gold refined by fire so that you may be rich; and white robes to clothe you and to keep the shame of your nakedness from being seen; and salve to anoint your eyes so that you may see. I reprove and discipline those whom I love. Be earnest, therefore, and repent. Listen! I am standing at the door, knocking; if you hear my voice and open the door, I will come in to you and eat with you and you with me. To the one who conquers I will give a place with me on my throne, just as I myself conquered and sat down with my Father on his throne. Let anyone who has an ear listen to what the Spirit is saying to the churches."

The Heavenly Temple (4:1-8)

Reader 1:

After this I looked, and there in heaven a door stood open! And the first voice, which I had heard speaking to me like a trumpet, said: "Come up here, and I will show you what must take place after this." At once I was in the spirit, and there in heaven stood a throne, with one seated on the throne! And the one seated there looks like jasper and carnelian, and around the throne is a rainbow that looks like an emerald. Around the throne are twenty-four thrones, and seated on the thrones are twenty-four elders, dressed in white robes, with golden crowns on their heads. Coming from the throne are flashes of lightning, and rumblings and peals of thunder, and in front of the throne burn seven flaming torches, which are the seven spirits of God; and in front of the throne there is something like a sea of glass, like crystal.

Around the throne, and on each side of the throne, are four living creatures, full of eyes in front and behind: the first living creature like a lion, the second living creature like an ox, the third living creature with a face like a human face, and the fourth living creature like an flying eagle. And the four living creatures, each of them with six wings, are full of eyes all around and inside. Day and night with ceasing they sing:

"Holy, holy, holy,
the Lord God the Almighty,
who was and is and is to come!"

The Lamb and the Scroll (5:1-8)

Reader 2:

Then I saw in the right hand of the one seated
on the throne a scroll written on the inside and
on the back, sealed with seven seals; and I saw
a mighty angel proclaiming with a loud voice:
"Who is worthy to open the scroll and break its
seals?" And no one in heaven or on earth or
under the earth was able to open the scroll or to
look into it. And I began to weep bitterly
because no one was found worthy to open the
scroll or to look into it. Then one of the elders
said to me: "Do not weep. See, the Lion of the
tribe of Judah, the Root of David, has
conquered, so that he can open the scroll and
its seven seals."

Then I saw between the throne and the four
living creatures and among the elders a Lamb
standing as if it had been slaughtered, having
seven horns and seven eyes, which are the
seven spirits of God sent out into all the earth.
He went and took the scroll from the right hand
of the one who was seated on the throne. When
he had taken the scroll, the four living creatures
and the twenty-four elders fell before the Lamb,
each holding a harp and golden bowls full of
incense, which are the prayers of the saints.

Hymn (5:9-10,11)

You are worthy to take the scroll
    and to open its seals,
for you were slaughtered and by your blood
    you ransomed for God

136

saints from every tribe and language and
people and nation;
You have made them to be a kingdom and
priests serving our God,
and they will reign on earth.

Worthy is the Lamb that was slaughtered
to receive power and wealth and wisdom and
might
and honor and glory and blessing!

The First Four Seals (6:1-8)

Reader 3:

Then I saw the Lamb open one of the seven
seals, and I heard one of the four living
creatures call out, as with a voice of thunder,
"Come!" I looked, and there was a white horse!
Its rider had a bow; a crown was given to him,
and he came out conquering and to conquer.
    When he opened the second seal, I heard the
second living creature call out, "Come!" And out
came another horse, bright red; its rider was
permitted to take peace from the earth, so that
people would slaughter one another; and he was
given given a great sword.
    When he opened the third seal, I heard the
third living creature call out, "Come!" I looked,
and there was a black horse! Its rider held a
pair of scales in his hand, and I heard what
seemed to be a voice in the midst of the four
living creatures saying, "A quart of wheat for a
day's pay, and three quarts of barley for a day's
pay, but do not damage the olive oil and the
wine!"

When he opened the fourth seal, I heard the voice of the fourth living creature call out, "Come!" I looked and there was a pale green horse! Its rider's name was Death, and Hades followed with him; they were given authority over a fourth of the earth, to kill with sword, famine, and pestilence, and by the wild animals of the earth.

The Fifth Seal (6:9-11)

Reader 4:

When he broke the fifth seal, I saw under the altar the souls of those who had been slaughtered for the word of God and for the testimony they had given; they cried out with a loud voice, "Sovereign Lord, holy and true, how long will it be before you judge and avenge our blood on the inhabitants of the earth?" They were each given a white robe and told to rest a little longer, until the number would be complete both of their fellow servants and of their brothers and sisters, who were soon to be killed as they themselves had been killed.

The Victors (7:9,13-17)

Reader 1:

After this I looked, and there was a great multitude that no one could count, from every nation, from all tribes and peoples and languages, standing before the throne and before the Lamb, robed in white, with palm branches in their hands.

Then one of the elders addressed me, saying, "Who are these, robed in white, and where have they come from?" I said to him, "Sir, you are the one who knows." Then he said to me, "They are they who have come out of the great ordeal; they have washed their robes and made them white in the blood of the Lamb.

"For this reason they are before the throne of
God,
and worship him day and night within his
temple,
and the one who is seated on the throne
will shelter them.
They will hunger no more, and thirst no more;
the sun will not strike them,
nor any scorching heat;
for the Lamb at the center of the throne will
be their shepherd,
and he will guide them to the springs of the
water of life;
and God will wipe away every tear from their
eyes."

Hymn (7:10,12)

Salvation belongs to our God who is seated on
the throne, and to the Lamb!

Amen! Blessing and glory and wisdom
and thanksgiving and honor
and power and might
be to our God forever and ever! Amen.

Woman and Dragon (12:1-9,13-17)

Reader 2:

A great portent appeared in heaven: a woman clothed with the sun, with the moon under her feet, and on her head a crown of twelve stars. She was pregnant and was crying out in birthpangs, in the agony of giving birth. Then another portent appeared in heaven: a great red dragon, with seven heads and ten horns and seven diadems on his heads. His tail swept down a third of the stars of heaven and threw them to the earth. Then the dragon stood before the woman who was about to bear a child, so that he might devour her child as soon as it was born. And she gave birth to a son, a male child, who is to rule all the nations with a rod of iron. But her child was snatched away and taken to God and to his throne; and the woman fled into the wilderness, where she has a place prepared by God, so that there she can be nourished for one thousand two hundred and sixty days.

And war broke out in heaven; Michael and his angels fought against the dragon. The dragon and his angels fought back, but they were defeated, and there was no longer any place for them in heaven. The great dragon was thrown down, that ancient serpent, who is called the Devil and Satan, the deceiver of the whole world—he was thrown down to the earth, and his angels were thrown down with him.

So when the dragon saw that he had been thrown down to the earth, he pursued the woman who had given birth to the male child. But the woman was given the two wings of the great eagle, so that she could fly from the serpent into the wilderness, to her place where

she is nourished for a time, and times, and half
a time. Then from his mouth the serpent poured
water like a river after the woman, to sweep her
away with the flood. But the earth came to the
help of the woman; it opened its mouth and
swallowed the river that the dragon had poured
from his mouth. Then the dragon was angry
with the woman, and went off to make war on
the rest of her children, those who keep the
commandments of God and hold the testimony
of Jesus.

Proclamation (12:10-12)

Presider:

Then I heard a loud voice in heaven,
proclaiming,

"Now have come the salvation and the power
and the kingdom of our God
and the authority of his Messiah,
for the accuser of our comrades has been
thrown down,
who accuses them day and night before our
God.
But they have conquered him by the blood of
the Lamb
and by the word of their testimony,
for they did not cling to life even in the face of
death.
Rejoice, then, you heavens
and those who dwell in them!
But woe to the earth and the sea,
for the devil has come down to you
with great wrath,
because he knows that his time is short!"

The Beasts (13:1-2,7-10,11-12,18)

Reader 3:

And I saw a beast rising out of the sea; and on its horns were ten diadems, and on its heads were blasphemous names. And the beast that I saw was like a leopard, its feet were like a bear's, and its mouth like a lion's mouth. And the dragon gave it his power and his throne and great authority.

Also it was allowed to make war on the saints and to conquer them. It was given authority over every tribe and people and language and nation, and all the inhabitants of the earth will worship it, everyone whose name has not been written from the foundation of the world in the book of life of the Lamb that was slaughtered.

Let anyone who has an ear listen:

If you are to be taken captive,
   into captivity you go;
if you kill with the sword,
   with the sword you must be killed.

Here is a call for the endurance and faith of the saints.

Then I saw another beast that rose out of the earth; it had two horns like a lamb and it spoke like a dragon. It exercises all the authority of the first beast on its behalf, and it makes the earth and its inhabitants worship the first beast, whose mortal wound had been healed. [L]et anyone with understanding calculate the number of the beast, for it is the number of a person. Its number is six hundred sixty-six.

Companions of the Lamb (14:1-5)

Reader 4:

Then I looked, and there was the Lamb,
standing on Mount Zion! And with him were one
hundred forty-four thousand who had his name
and his Father's name written on their
foreheads. And I heard a voice from heaven like
the sound of many waters and like the sound of
loud thunder; the voice I heard was like the
sound of harpists playing on their harps, and
they sing a new song before the throne and the
four living creatures and before the elders. No
one could learn that song except the one
hundred forty-four thousand who have been
redeemed from the earth....[T]hese follow the
Lamb wherever he goes. They have been
redeemed from humankind as first fruits for
God and the Lamb, and in their mouth no lie
was found; they are blameless.

Hymn (15:3-4)

Great and amazing are your deeds,
   Lord God the Almighty!
Just and true are your ways,
   King of the nations!

Lord, who will not fear
   and glorify your name?
For you alone are holy.
   All nations will come
   and worship before you,
for your judgments have been revealed.

The Harlot (17:1-6)

Reader 1:

Then one of the seven angels who had the seven bowls came and said to me: "Come, I will show you the judgment of the great whore who is seated on many waters, with whom the kings of the earth have committed fornication, and with the wine of whose fornication the inhabitants of the earth have become drunk." So he carried me away in the spirit into a wilderness, and I saw a woman sitting on a scarlet beast that was full of blasphemous names, and it had seven heads and ten horns. The woman was clothed in purple and scarlet, and adorned with gold and jewels and pearls, holding in her hand a golden cup full of abominations and the impurities of her fornication; and on her forehead was written a name, a mystery: "Babylon the great, mother of whores and of earths' abominations." And I saw that the woman was drunk with the blood of the saints and the blood of the witnesses to Jesus.
    When I saw her, I was greatly amazed.

End of Babylon (18:1-2,21)

Presider:

After this I saw another angel coming down from heaven, having great authority; and the earth was made bright with his splendor. He called out with a mighty voice,

    "Fallen, fallen is Babylon the great!

Then a mighty angel took up a stone like a great millstone and threw it into the sea, saying:

With such violence Babylon the great city
will be thrown down,
and will be found no more....

End of Evil (19:11-16,19-21)

Reader 1:

Then I saw heaven opened, and there was a
white horse! Its rider is called Faithful and True,
and in righteousness he judges and makes war.
His eyes are like a flame of fire, and on his head
are many diadems; and he has a name inscribed
that no one knows but himself. He is clothed in
a robe dipped in blood, and his name is called
The Word of God. And the armies of heaven,
wearing fine linen, white and pure, were
following him on white horses. From his mouth
comes a sharp sword with which to strike down
the nations, and he will rule them with a rod of
iron; he will tread the winepress of the fury of
the wrath of God the Almighty. On his robe and
on his thigh he has a name inscribed, "King of
kings and Lord of lords."

Then I saw the beast and the kings of the
earth with their armies gathered make war
against the rider on the horse and against his
army. And the beast was captured, and with it
the false prophet who had performed in its
presence the signs by which he deceived those
who had received the mark of the beast and
those who worshiped its image. These two were
thrown alive into the lake of fire that burns with
sulfur. And the rest were killed by the sword of
the rider on the horse, the sword that came
from his mouth....

Hymn (19:6-8)

Hallelujah!
For the Lord our God
    the Almighty reigns.
Let us rejoice and exult
    and give him the glory,
for the marriage of the Lamb has come,
    and his bride has made herself ready;
to her it is granted to be clothed
    with fine linen, bright and pure"—

for the fine linen is the righteousness deeds of
the saints.

Last Judgment (20:11-15)

Reader 2:

Then I saw a great white throne and the one
who sat on it; the earth and the heaven fled
from his presence, and no place was found for
them. And I saw the dead, great and small,
standing before the throne, and books were
opened. Also another book was opened, the
book of life. And the dead were judged according
to their works, as recorded in the books. And
the sea gave up the dead that were in it, Death
and Hades gave up the dead that were in them,
and all were judged according to what they had
done. Then Death and Hades were thrown into
the lake of fire. This is the second death, the
lake of fire; and anyone whose name was not
found written in the book of life was thrown into
the lake of fire.

The New Jerusalem
(21:1-3,9-12,14,22-26)

Reader 3:

Then I saw a new heaven and a new earth; for
the first heaven and the first earth had passed
away, and the sea was no more. And I saw the
holy city, the new Jerusalem, coming down out
of heaven from God, prepared as a bride
adorned for her husband. And I heard a loud
voice from the throne saying,

> "See, the home of God is among mortals.
> He will dwell with them as their God;
> they will be his peoples,
> and God himself will be with them...."

Then one of the seven angels who had the
seven bowls full of the seven last plagues came
and said to me, "Come. I will show you the
bride, the wife of the Lamb." And in the spirit he
carried me away to a great, high mountain and
showed me the holy city Jerusalem coming
down out of heaven from God. It has the glory of
God and a radiance like a very rare jewel, like
jasper, clear as crystal. It has a great, high wall
with twelve gates, and at the gates twelve
angels, and on the gates are inscribed the
names of the twelve tribes of the Israelites....And
the wall of the city has twelve foundations, and
on them are the twelve names of the twelve
apostles of the Lamb.

I saw no temple in the city, for its temple is
the Lord God the Almighty and the Lamb. And
the city has no need of sun or moon to shine on
it, for the glory of God is its light, and its lamp is
the Lamb. The nations will walk by its light, and
the kings of the earth will bring their glory into

it. Its gates will never be shut by day—and there will be no night there. People will bring into it the glory and the honor of the nations.

Hymn (21:3-4)

See, the home of God is among mortals.
He will dwell with them as their God;
they will be his peoples,
and God himself will be with them;
he will wipe every tear from their eyes.
Death will be no more;
mourning and crying and pain will be no
  more,
for the first things have passed away.

Epilogue (22:16,20)

Presider:

"It is I, Jesus, who sent my angel to you with this testimony for the churches. I am the root and the descendant of David, the bright morning star."

The one who testifies to these things says: "Surely I am coming soon!"

Assembly:

Amen! Come, Lord Jesus!

Final Blessing (22:21)

Presider:

The grace of the Lord Jesus be with all.

Glossary

apocalypse. A literary genre or form. The kind of literature in which apocalyptic viewpoints are expressed.

apocalyptic eschatology. God is guiding history to an End that is very near. The divine plan involves the vindication of the alienated suffering ones.

apocalypticism. The world-view of an apocalyptic movement or group. In practice it is a view of the marginalized: "God is on our side."

emperor-cult. In the Roman Empire, especially in the Eastern Christian provinces, the Emperor was worshiped as a deity. Christian refusal to worship the Emperor could be regarded as political dissent.

eschatology. God is guiding history to a determined End. Greek *eschaton* = end.

millenialism. Based on a literal interpretation of Revelation 20:1-10, millenialism has taken many forms. One way or another, it posits an earthly thousand-year reign of the elect with Christ before the End.

Nicolaitans. Named only in Revelation 2:6,15. Nicolaitanism seems to be a tendency in the churches of the province of Asia firmly rejected by the author of Revelation.

premillenial dispensationalism. A brand of fundamentalist eschatology, notably prevalent in the United States. The term "dispensationalism" refers to the theory that God "dispenses" or administers the divine purpose throughout history in seven successive stages called "dispensations." The seventh dispensation is that of the millennium (Rev 20:1-10).

Resources

Commentaries

Boring, M. Eugene. *Revelation: Interpretation.* Louisville: John Knox, 1989.

Caird, G.B. *The Revelation of St. John the Divine.* New York: Harper & Row, 1966.

Collins, A. Yarbro. *The Apocalypse.* New Testament Message Series, vol. 22. Wilmington, Delaware: M. Glazier, 1979.

————. "Apocalypse (Revelation)." 996-1016. *New Jerome Biblical Commentary.* New Jersey: Prentice Hall, 1990.

Fiorenza, E. Schüssler. *Invitation to the Book of Revelation.* New York: Doubleday, 1981.

Harrington, W. J. *Revelation.* Sacra Pagina Series, vol. 16. Collegeville: Liturgical Press, 1993.

Kealy, S. P. *The Apocalypse of John.* Wilmington, Delaware: M. Glazier, 1987.

Krodel, G. A., *Revelation.* Minneapolis: Augsburg, 1989.

Minear, P. S. *I Saw a New Earth.* Washington: Corpus, 1968.

Morris, L. *Revelation.* Grand Rapids: Eerdmans, 1969.

Mounce, R. H. *The Book of Revelation.* Grand Rapids: Eerdmans, 1977.

Sweet, J. P. M. *Revelation.* Pelican Commentaries. Philadelphia: Westminster, 1979.

Studies

Collins, A. Yarbro. *Crisis and Catharsis: The Power of the Apocalypse.* Philadelphia: Westminster, 1984.

Collins, J. J. *The Apocalyptic Imagination: An Introduction to the Jewish Matrix of Christianity.* New York: Crossroad, 1987.

Court, J. *Myth and History in the Book of Revelation.* Atlanta: John Knox, 1979.

Fiorenza, E. Schüssler. *The Book of Revelation: Justice and Judgment.* Philadelphia: Fortress, 1985.

Guthrie, D. *The Relevance of John's Apocalypse.* Grand Rapids: Eerdmans, 1987.

Hanson, P. D. *The Dawn of Apocalyptic.* Philadelphia: Fortress, 1978.

Hemer, C. J. *The Letters to the Seven Churches of Asia in their Local Setting.* Sheffield: *Journal for the Study of the New Testament,* 1986.

Minear, P. S. *New Testament Apocalyptic.* Nashville: Abingdon, 1981.

Rowland, C. *The Open Heaven: A Study of Apocalyptic in Judaism and Christianity.* New York: Crossroad, 1982.

Thompson, L. L. *The Book of Revelation: Apocalypse and Empire.* New York: Oxford University Press, 1990.

Index of Scripture References

Index of Scripture References

Index of Topics